Russian Reform/
International Money

The Lionel Robbins Lectures

Russian Reform/
International Money

Yegor Gaidar
Karl Otto Pöhl

The MIT Press
Cambridge, Massachusetts
London, England

This book was set in Palatino by Compset, Inc. and was printed and bound
in the United States of America.

Library of Congress Cataloging-in-Publication Data

Gaidar, E. T. (Egor Timurovich)
  Russian reform/International money / Yegor Gaidar, Karl Otto Pöhl.
    p.   cm. — (The Lionel Robbins lectures)
  Includes index.
  ISBN 0-262-07165-7
  1. Soviet Union—Economic policy—1986-1991. 2. Russia
(Federation—Economic policy—1991- 3. Economic assistance—Soviet
Union. 4. Economic assistance—Russia (Federation)
5. International finance. 6. Monetary policy—Europe. I. Pöhl,
Karl Otto, 1929- . II. Title. III. Series.
HC336.26.G353   1995
338.947—dc20   94-45868
                                                              CIP

Contents

Foreword

In the last decade the face of Europe has changed beyond recognition. Two changes dominate all others: the economic reforms in the East and the growing economic and monetary integration of the West.

In 1993 the London School of Economics therefore invited as Lionel Robbins Memorial Lecturers two giant figures who have been at the center of these events: Yegor Gaidar (former prime minister of the Federation of Russia) and Karl Otto Pöhl (former president of the Deutsche Bundesbank).

Each of these men has changed the world we live in. Yegor Gaidar launched the economic reform effort in Russia in 1992 and has played a key role in its evolution. Karl Otto Pöhl, more than anyone, turned back the great European inflation of the 1970s and 1980s and laid the framework for future monetary stability in Europe.

Both are distinguished not only for their actions but for their intellectual power and clarity of vision. It is therefore fascinating to see how they perceived the problems as they arose (with all the uncertainties and risks involved) and how they used basic economic analysis to chart their course.

Richard Layard
London School of Economics

Russian Reform

Yegor Gaidar

1   Our Inheritance

I shall begin by discussing our inheritance: the economic situation existing when we came to power in November 1991. This background is essential to understanding our strategy and makes theoretical arguments about shock treatment versus gradualism largely irrelevant. It is very easy to make a case for gradualism by comparing the experience of China or Vietnam (with their rapidly expanding production, social stability, and GDP growth of more than 10% per year) with the experiences of Russia and Eastern Europe, which are going through a very difficult period of structural transformation. It is also not difficult to make the opposite case by contrasting the experience of the different countries of the former Soviet Union and Eastern Europe. In this case it is clear that those who tried the gradual approach are now worse off. This is especially true in the case of the Ukraine and Romania, whereas those countries that were leaders in the reform process, like Poland or Czechoslovakia, are now showing the strongest rates of economic growth.

Obviously this debate cannot be resolved by applying the Orwellian principle of two legs good, four legs bad, or vice versa. It will go on for years, and I will not try to pretend that I am going to settle it. But I would like to draw attention to the practical points that are relatively clear from my point of view.

First, no previous communist or totalitarian government had ever tried shock treatment. Probably the closest attempt was launched by Mieczyslaw Rakovski's government in Poland in 1989 without, in fact, any notable success. But neither had any government, democratic or communist, ever tried the gradualist approach with any success either. The governments of Romania and the Ukraine are probably the best examples of gradualism, a course they followed for political reasons. In fact, I would say that the gradualist approach to transforming a communist economy is the strategy of a communist or totalitarian regime trying to adapt to new realities—probably the only politically feasible option for this kind of regime. Such a strategy is not without the possibility of success, especially if undertaken at an early stage of the country's development and along very liberal lines. But shock treatment is usually the only alternative for a postcommunist government coming to power after the strategy of the previous regime (or bad luck) has led to the failure of the gradualist approach. So in practice there is often little choice of strategy for any one type of political regime, for the political and economic situation dictates which kind of economic policy can be promoted.

When Mikhail Gorbachev came to power in 1985, any serious discussion of shock treatment or radical economic reform was, from a political point of view, absolutely out of the question. Soviet society was very stable, and practically all levels of society believed that this stability would last for decades. If you tried to make someone take seriously the suggestion that in ten years the Soviet Union would disappear, and that we would be living in a privatized economy, it would not even have been funny; it would simply not have been a topic for discussion.

Gorbachev's greatest political strength was his ability to achieve compromise in his management of the ruling elite. It was fascinating to see how he managed the big meetings attended by leaders of the regions, party organizations, big factories, and branch ministries. When some serious issue of economic policy was being discussed, he manipulated the discussion so that the decision reached somehow appeared to be the one favored by the majority—and he would act as if he were accepting their decision. It was a very interesting art, but it created serious problems for the political leader who practiced it. It meant he could not stray too far from the real preferences of the political elite. He had to follow events, and he had to follow problems. He could not go a few steps ahead of the situation.

In 1985 therefore Russia was very stable, and this stability was all the more striking in that it permeated society as a whole, from the point of view of macroeconomics, money, and society generally. The rate of money growth was quite stable and, although a budget deficit existed, it was at a low level. Short-term periods of increased inflationary pressures, the latest of which was seen around 1978/79, could usually be eliminated by raising the prices of luxury items, exerting tighter control over wages, and increasing import taxes on consumer durables.

It was a society with a very static economic structure. For example, the distribution of investment in the different branches of the economy remained the same from year to year. If, for instance, it was usual to allot 26% of investment to agriculture, that figure would have been the same in 1970 or 1975, in 1980 or 1989. The most striking example of this was the rate of investment in the big water redistribution and irrigation projects. Each year we used to spend approximately the same amount of money on irrigation projects that was invested in the civil machine-building industry and approximately, for example, ten times more than investment in communications. For twenty years there was no visible improvement in the harvest as a result of this huge irrigation project, but it was completely out of the question to reduce, even by a few people, this investment because this was how it had been done a year ago, two years ago, five years ago, and ten years ago.

This was a society in which the stability of prices, especially of basic consumer commodities, was almost a religious belief for the ruling elite. This was a consequence of events in 1962 when the communist government decided to slightly increase prices for meat and milk products, resulting in the first serious riots on Russian territory during communist rule. The idea that you could not touch the price of basic commodities was simply not in dispute from a political point of view. After the events in Poland in the 1970s, when the Gomulka government was involved in the increase in meat prices, it was forbidden to even discuss the question of a change in the price of consumer goods.

This continued to create serious problems for the economy. Society and the ruling elite had to pay more and more for this stability, for this immobility of the economy. The most obvious result was the constant increase in subsidies as a share of GDP, which approached 8% at the beginning of 1985. Increases in agricultural imports had to be financed by oil exports. Despite this rise, and a growing shortage of consumer goods due to increased demand, stability could not be undermined for any reason.

It was also evident that the country was once more losing its long-term economic competitiveness against the more dynamic and rapidly developing economies of the world. The Russian construction industry was uncompetitive in the world market. Keeping oil production even constant posed more and more of a problem from the point of view of investment. Agriculture was in a state of long-term crisis; the enormous investment in this sector during the twenty years between 1965 and 1985 had produced very unimpressive results. But, as long as it seemed that society and the economy were stable, nothing really pushed the ruling elite to change anything. If this strategy of price stability were to be maintained, however, it meant that the gap between the most developed countries and Russia would widen steadily. That was the main point of discussion among the ruling elite at the time of Gorbachev's nomination. Should we rely increasingly on the great innovation of the previous generation—stability—or should we try once more to catch up with the rapidly growing Western economies?

For the third time Russia was confronted with the problem of catching up, each time with very serious long-term political and economic consequences. The first time was at the end of the 1870s. It was evident that the abolition of serfdom by itself would not provide the necessary inputs that would encourage the rapid development of the Russian economy. In that period Russia faced for the first time what would prove to be its most serious long-term economic problem: the low level of private savings and private investment. The peasants were tied in to *obshina* (the system of communes), and without a clear profit derived from the land or from incomes, and with the very specific tax base that was practically a tax on efficient production, they were not stimulated to save or invest. The gentry, with its long-term tradition of conspicuous consumption, was not going to be the source of the flow of savings for this economy. A weak budget undermined the possibility of bringing in foreign investment on a large scale. Russia once more applied the idea of investment financed by huge governmental savings and governmental investment based on an increase in business taxation, which was used to finance railroad construction and the creation of national industries protected by import barriers. So Russia embarked on the road of government-led import substitution and thus industrialization.

It was considered an economic success, but success combined with enormous social risks because it was partly based on excessive taxation of an impoverished countryside. The slogan of this period was "We will not eat enough, but we will export." Russian grain export was the basis of the establishment of the country's gold reserves and financial stability. But this was taking place alongside an impending peasant revolt. Which would come first? Between the years 1907 and 1913, after the first Russian revolution, it looked as if the development of national confidence would succeed. But history proved otherwise, and the country of burgeoning capitalism and impoverished peasants could not survive World War I. The Russian revolution was in part a result of this strategy of government-led industrialization.

The second time Russia was faced with this same question was at the end of the 1920s when, after the communist revolution, it was beset with problems very similar to those that had existed before the big financial reforms of the late nineteenth century. Russian emigré literature of the 1920s and the professional journals of the 1920s in Russia reflected a widespread view that what was happening was capitalist development under socialist slogans. The major part of the economy consisted, of course, of the peasant countryside and small-scale industry. A market was operating. It was restricted, but it operated all the same. The most serious problem once more was one of private saving and private investment. Given the prevailing socialist ideology, it was useless to hope for huge savings and investment from the peasantry faced with the prospect of being classed as political enemies and subject to political oppression for engaging in such activities. The same was true of urban entrepreneurs. The political instability of the situation created strong incentives for them to indulge in short-term operations, not long-term investments. And it was hopeless to expect foreign investment after the repudiation of the czar's debts. It was also very unlikely that state industry would be a serious source of investment, when for political reasons the increase in wages of the urban proletariat was much higher than the increase in productivity.

Stalin was therefore faced with a dilemma, and he reacted with a very bold and innovative plan that had an enormous influence on the general development of the world economy in the twentieth century. In a market economy there are very obvious limits on the amount of governmental saving. For example, if you are financing enormous governmental saving with high taxes, then high taxes have strong negative influences on the general level of economic activity. If you are financing excessive governmental saving from inflationary sources, then inflation by itself encourages the flight of capital and discourages long-term investment. In this way we remove the micro instruments of a market economy.

So Stalin integrated all Soviet enterprises into big hierarchical structures. Under this system enterprises buy and sell goods not because they want to but because they are ordered to. Therefore investments are no longer dependent on stimuli but rather on the decisions of the government. Strong financial control prevents capital flight. Eliminating the huge inequality that is characteristic of young capitalism or of the old totalitarian regime gives some additional legitimacy to this policy. And all this is combined with totalitarian political control, which prevents wage increases and any independent trade union activity. In effect it makes development dependent on internal saving. It's a type of governmental-led growth that can be sustained to a rather high level for a long period of time.

If we look back at this type of growth we can see how appalling it is. It offers the possibility of short-term success but destroys the economic structure in the long term. It creates the possibility of high economic growth, but it also creates enormous long-term problems that have to be dealt with later. First, it eliminates the source of an independent flow of innovation created by micro market mechanisms. Then it leads to tremendous bureaucratization of the entire economic system because an enormous bureaucracy is needed to conduct the day-to-day transactions that would otherwise be made by the market. This bureaucratization creates difficulties in coordinating economic activity. When you develop complicated industrial structures in which every transaction is made not because of economic stimuli but because of a governmental order, you are faced with huge organizational problems. You try to avoid these problems by minimizing change—avoiding any innovation if at all possible and stabilizing all elements of the economy. So any branch of the economy that is created usually survives. The slogan used to describe the problems connected with inefficient industries and enterprises in Russia is: "This is not a private kiosk."

Even if the enterprise is inefficient and its products are absolutely useless, it does not mean that the enterprise should be closed or its resources redistributed; rather it is part of the state organization and therefore must be protected and supplied. After the first stage of industrialization, when the basics of the industrial structure were formed, no industry in Russia ever had its resources redistributed to other industries; production would not cease simply because there was no longer a demand for the products or because a more efficient way had been found to produce them. Once an industry was set up, it became part of the state apparatus and was entitled to its share of the assets. This type of economy could be dynamic and have a high level of growth, but only until its resources were needed elsewhere to create a new industry.

One source in particular—the countryside—was deprived of its culture and converted to collective and state agriculture. The countryside had provided the financial and material resources that were used during the period of industrialization. When these resources are available (for instance, in China they were present at the beginning of the recent reforms), you have a rather dynamic developing economy. In Russia, when it became clear that there were no more resources in the countryside that could be accumulated through state ownership and used in industrialization, the crisis of relying on this model of economic growth began. From this moment on, especially when the need for further investment in agriculture became evident, it was obvious that this structure was static and simply would not develop any further.

In 1985 the basic characteristics of the situation were more or less obvious to Soviet policymakers. It was also clear that it was useless to try to resolve the traditional Russian problem in the traditional Russian way by using additional governmental savings and investment, because the problems were on both the macro and micro levels. All of the difficulties were connected to the fact that without market mechanisms you cannot fight an increasing paralysis of the economic mechanism, with its predictable sclerotic outcome.

Thus it was fairly evident what the Gorbachev government should have done if it wanted to introduce a strategy of gradualist transformation. First, it should have tried to preserve financial stability, which was the strongest pillar of the economic system. It should also have tried to protect, for the time being at least, existing levels of governmental saving and investment, and incorporate step-by-step the new market mechanisms that would make the system work, to make them more adaptable and innovative.

I am not certain whether it was possible at the time to use this strategy successfully. But the political elite's first actions were completely in the opposite direction. Once more, they chose to use old-style solutions for Russia's problems of growth.

What were the most obvious problems? First, there was a slowdown of economic growth. Why was there a slowdown? Gorbachev and his advisers concluded it was because the old guard had failed to enforce discipline, for example, by prohibiting drunkenness in the work force. Insufficient investment was also a tremendous problem; more should have been invested in machine building, agriculture, the energy sector, etc. It was clear that the old guard was unable to do anything, but now younger and more energetic individuals were prepared to take action.

So with their first strokes the Gorbachev government undermined the basic foundation of financial stability that had been maintained in Russia since 1947: taxes were placed on alcohol, and the level of government expenditure on investment increased. The attempt to increase the rate of investment approximately three times between 1985 and 1986 created enormous financial imbalances. By 1987 financial stability was a thing of the past; the budget deficit had risen from 1% of GDP to almost 7%. There was a very rapid increase in money creation, and the result in the consumer goods market was the development of acute shortages. Goods that had been in easy supply on the market for decades, such as spoons and detergent, were eliminated one by one from the shelves. It was clear by 1987 that the government's first attempt to increase the rate of growth by additional investment was not producing results.

Obviously there were problems in the economic mechanisms; the economy simply was not functioning well. In 1987, however, the use of words such as market or liberalization or terms like liberalization of prices were absolutely out of the question for discussion among the political elite. And as I have said, this placed Gorbachev in a difficult position. He could not discuss problems that were very much out of the reach of the political elite.

What were the subjects usually addressed by the political elite when discussing problems at the micro level? As in the army, there are crucial jobs; for instance, in the Russian army, the job of the regiment commander is extremely important. Anyone aspiring to a military career must first be a regiment commander or he will not go far. A comparable job exists in the Russian civilian hierarchy: the role of the enterprise director. A party secretary or a branch minister of the regional party committee should, at least for a short period of time, have been an enterprise director. It is the position in which the *nomenklatura* (for the briefest possible time) are in contact with real life. The experience of the enterprise director creates his model for dealing with the economy. An enterprise director has his own ideas of what really constitutes a problem in the economy. Naturally, he is dissatisfied with the fact that profit is being redistributed and that he cannot have control of it himself. At the same time, of course, he feels that if he is running a deficit the state should compensate him for these losses. But what really constitutes a problem for him is that he is not free to do with his products what he would like; he cannot sell to those who from his point of view would be the most suitable buyers. On the other hand, he would expect the state to arrange things so that those who have to sell their products to him will not try to sell them to someone else. Therefore, if you wanted to speak about economic reform in terms of price liberalization being introduced into the market, you would be confronting the political elite. Should you put things in a way that suggested increasing the powers of the enterprise directors, however, you would get enormous support. Everyone would agree with you.

Therefore the next stage of economic transformation, which was discussed in 1987 and implemented in 1989, was the reform of state management that resulted in an increase in the powers of the state enterprise directors. With regard to the law relating to state enterprises, a very unusual situation was developing that represented a terrible blow to the most basic principles of the old hierarchical economy. Until now, members of the hierarchy were in a state of complete dependence on their bosses; state orders had to be fulfilled. Now, acceptance of state orders was voluntary; the enterprise director could either take them or refuse them. Some portion of the profits would not be redistributed by the state; it would remain with the enterprise, giving the enterprise director some very specific property rights. He could not even be dismissed without the collective's workers first being asked if they were prepared to support his dismissal. All this had an effect on the working of the Russian economy as if, for example, you had tried to introduce a military law establishing the right of the regimental commander to sell the country's military equipment, to dispose freely of the income, to choose against whom he would like to fight, and then make it impossible to dismiss him until the entire regiment supported his dismissal. With this increased decentralization the means of managing repressed inflation were removed.

First, financial stability was destroyed and the level of repressed inflation was increased, as was the level of shortages. Then, in the second stage, the mechanisms that had been especially set up in the socialist economy to deal with repressed inflation were themselves being destroyed. It is hardly surprising that the results were disastrous, since the alternative mechanisms—liberalized prices, the system of the markets, property rights, etc.—were absent. Formally, prices were fixed. There was a traditional belief that the enterprises took some notice of the branch ministries, at least some of the time, and that regional party organizations could exert some authority over them. But, as time went on, their influence became weaker and weaker. So from 1989 onward the possibility of managing the economy was becoming less and less likely, and the number of distortions was on the rise.

Gorbachev was in a very difficult position. It was obvious to everyone that something was wrong. He was apparently making all the right moves. Every action was supported by the political elite, every step was absolutely right; but somehow the results were disastrous. You could no longer buy goods in Russian shops, and the situation continued to deteriorate. Somebody had to take responsibility. At the highest levels of the party organization there was a feeling that Gorbachev was allowing too much freedom of the press. Gorbachev remembered all too well the experience of one of his energetic predecessors, Nikita Khrushchev, who had been dismissed by the plenum of the Central Committee. If you were in touch with high-ranking party officials at that time, you could feel the hatred they harbored for Gorbachev and even sense that preparations were under way to remove him. So he decided at once to take an enormous political leap by creating a new political base for himself. This base would no longer be the party organization as it had been before, but rather a semi-democratic parliament that would support the first democratic Russian president, or chairman of the Soviet.

This was the beginning of a large-scale political reform movement that altered the distribution of power in Soviet society. The change coincided with an enormous economic crisis that was widely felt. From an economic standpoint, the first and most obvious result of these steps toward political liberalization was an explosion of social expectations. The first slogans of those who were being promoted to the people's deputies in the first free Russian elections promised everything with no costs. They promised to cut taxes, drastically increase expenditure on all social needs (including pensions and health care), maintain subsidies, and increase consumer goods prices. Predictably, after the 1989 elections, the result was an explosion in social expenditure. Any attempt to control the budget after this would be fruitless.

The third phase in Gorbachev's economic policy was the implementation of economic reforms in the midst of a very serious economic crisis. After this it was fairly obvious that any serious discussion about a gradual transformation of the Russian economy was out of the question. There was no longer any real way of controlling the flow of resources in the economy, or the financial flows for that matter. The economy was developing rapidly in the direction of barter trade. This period was significant for the great number of Russian economic reform programs that were launched. From the end of 1989 until the summer of 1991, approximately fifteen economic reform programs were officially released, discussed, and usually adopted without having any serious effects on economic behavior or economic life. Furthermore, the programs' lack of effectiveness was evident to everybody.

The result of the economic crisis was a further division of power. The union's lack of power and the increasing economic turmoil created an enormous opportunity for the republics to grab power. Especially serious for the Russian economy was the battle now being waged for popularity between the new Russian government and the parliament and the union government and its parliament. In this fight, which was especially important in 1991, each group tried to adopt the most popular solution. The union parliament adopted a law that substantially increased the level of pensions; in response, the Russian government adopted an even more generous pension law. The union government cut the profit tax from 55% to 45%; the Russian parliament followed by cutting it to 38%; the union government then reduced it to 35%; and finally the Russian parliament cut it to 32%. There were similar developments in other aspects of economic life, making it absolutely impossible to manage the economy.

The union government clearly had no idea how to deal with the situation. It took extreme measures such as attempting monetary reform at the beginning of 1991, which resulted in the confiscation of approximately 3% of all cash money, drastically undermining the demand for money and the public's confidence in monetary stability and creating enormous additional inflationary consequences. In the aftermath of long negotiations, it was evident that the financial situation could not be resolved. In April 1991, the union government took responsibility for the first increase of consumer goods prices in thirty years. But it was not even able to collect the additional income the price increases generated. So three months later, in July, the balance of supply and demand in the consumer goods market remained unchanged.

The failed coup in August 1991 was an attempt by the old elite to remedy the situation: to drastically change it by reintroducing the old mechanisms of political, economic, and financial control and, in so doing, to turn back the clock. The coup's failure greatly altered the situation. The first result was the complete destruction of everything that was left from the previous mechanisms of governmental control. Until August, it had only been possible to manage the economy at all because the regional party committee's power was relatively strong at the micro level; they still managed to obtain some resources from the enterprises. But after August, the party committees had no possibility of doing anything. The same was true of the union ministries. The Russian government ran only approximately 7% of the Russian economy: the rest was run by the union ministries. After the coup, the legitimacy of the union ministries involved in the coup was nil. So nothing worked; furthermore, the Russian government had no legitimacy from the point of view of the regional soviets in which the Communists were the majority. It simply did not have the means necessary to manage the economy.

In Russia, political and economic crises usually manifest themselves by a crisis in the bread supply to the big cities.

So it was in 1917, the year of both the February and October revolutions, and so it was again at the end of the 1920s. The first obvious result of the August coup was a drop in the amount of grain bought by the state procurement organization. In the week following the coup, grain purchases fell by approximately four times compared with the weeks before the coup. We were approaching a very severe crisis in the supply of grain and bread to the big cities, and it was quite difficult to see how best to manage it. Any attempt to use the old-style mechanisms would have been useless. In this situation, any discussion of taking a gradual approach to Russian economic reform also would have been meaningless.

2   Liberalization

Immediately after the coup, the Russian leadership seemed strangely passive. It seemed that with victory won and the enemy destroyed, political and economic reforms would gain rapid momentum. Contrary to expectations, however, from September to mid-October very little was accomplished in Russia in the way of reforms. It is not difficult to understand why. The democrats were greatly surprised by their victory. They had had a very stable world in which they had a strong enemy—the Communist party, the union center—against whom they were prepared to fight for a long time. Following the coup they developed a system of uneasy alliances with other republican leaders who wanted to increase their own power, popularity, and prestige. They were fighting for improved Russian relationships abroad and for at least some recognition of their sovereignty by the G-7 countries.

The coalition that formed the basis of President Boris Yeltsin's electoral success was a very broad populist anti-communist coalition in which various forces ranging from true liberals to radical nationalists and even fascists were incorporated. Within a few months it was evident that this coalition would not survive the beginning of the economic reforms. During their political battles with the communists, the coalition promised a great deal to the Russian people including greater expenditure on social problems, no price increases, and various kinds of protection. Now, all at once on 22 August 1991, the responsibility for fulfilling these promises was transferred to President Yeltsin's shoulders. Technically, there was something left of the union government; but in the public consciousness of the average Russian citizen, Yeltsin was now responsible for everything that happened in Russia. He was responsible for the shortages, the lack of food, and especially the long queues for bread. The more intelligent communists were not at all dissatisfied with this situation. They believed that in a few months the democrats, unable to deal with Russia's difficult economic and social problems, would lose all of their popularity and that the people once more would invite back the old forces from the communist *nomenklatura*. And there was a real danger that this could be the outcome, because it was very difficult to confront the situation with any sensible, realistic political and economic strategy.

What exactly was Yeltsin confronting on 22 August? What was the real situation of the economy and society? First, it was quite clear that the old system of management no longer worked. The harvest had been bad, and a crisis in the ability of the state to purchase grain became increasingly evident after August. The grain reserves that had accumulated in the period before August would last only until about the beginning of January. Therefore, the problem of supplying bread to the large Russian cities had to be dealt with soon. There had been difficulties distributing the state grain reserves from the regions even when grain was relatively abundant—for example, from Stavropol, Krasnodar, and Rostov to areas suffering the most serious shortages such as Moscow and St. Petersburg—because the regional authorities prohibited their redistribution. Orders were no longer being handled efficiently, and trade was not working either.

The most pressing problems in Russian industry in the autumn of 1991 probably related to metals and coking coal; the miners would only provide coking coal to the metallurgical plants in exchange for metals. The miners would try to exchange the metals, for example, for automobiles produced in Togliatti, and then would try to exchange the automobiles for foodstuffs. This did not work too badly for the miners, but for the oil producers who have only one consumer—the petrochemical plants—it was very difficult to get the metal necessary for continuing oil production because it was now in the hands of the miners. The economy was unstable and unmanageable and was becoming seriously distorted. There were supply problems in the most basic branches of the national economy. For instance, it was extremely difficult to barter electroenergy for different kinds of goods, yet the electroenergy industry could not survive without spare parts.

In spite of this very difficult situation, branches of industry that were absolutely unnecessary at a time of such civil crisis continued to operate. For example, enormous amounts of metal and energy continued to be used in the production of military equipment, even though there were major problems with the heating systems in Moscow and St. Petersburg. Long-term investment projects, whose results were completely unpredictable, continued to operate. As a result, the crisis increased. Industrial production was down approximately 12% from its highest level in 1989, and the drop continued without any constructive changes in the system of economic management.

By September, the population was prepared for catastrophic disruptions in the food supply, in transportation, and in the availability of heat in the large urban areas. It can be seen from the press and television coverage of the period that there were no discussions, for instance, on what the best possible rate of inflation or the most sensible strategy of economic reform was; rather, attention focused on whether the country would survive the coming winter. That was the question on most people's minds.

What were the possible instruments that were available to Yeltsin? It is worth remembering that even after the August coup, union institutions still formally existed. They were totally inefficient and, in any case, no longer had legitimacy. Attempts were even being made to redistribute some of the union government's property to its employees.

The Soviet army had been strongly influenced by the August coup and the events of the previous two years. Several times before the coup, the civil leadership would issue orders for repressive measures to be carried out and then refuse to accept responsibility for them—putting the blame on the army. After the coup, the universal feeling in the army was that it did not want to interfere in politics, and it would not support oppression. This was the period during which Soviet military institutions were at their weakest—a period in which it was possible, for instance, for military equipment to be taken or stolen from the army without any serious repercussions. Thus the army could not be listed among the instruments at the disposal of the new Russian government. The army wanted to remain neutral and refused any order in connection with resolving internal conflicts. A similar stance was adopted by the Ministry of the Interior, although it was not quite as extreme. It also refused to sanction any force intended to resolve internal political conflicts.

In most of the republics and other regions of Russia, there were strong communist majorities on the local councils. The union government schemed with the regional governments in trying to create a coalition against Yeltsin. The legitimacy of the federal Russian government from the point of view of the local soviet was very limited. So there was great uncertainty as to whether they would comply with any orders from Moscow. Russian and union legislation also came into conflict, giving the enterprises and local authorities an excuse for not fulfilling any orders that came from Moscow. That meant that if Yeltsin tried to adopt a strategy of enforcing orders by emergency rule—for example, forcing the regions to supply food to Moscow and St. Petersburg—he did not have the means needed to implement the orders. I am absolutely sure that any attempt in the autumn of 1991 to introduce emergency laws and to make the regions obey orders from Moscow would have been a prologue to the disintegration of Russia and the outbreak of civil war. The effort to introduce emergency laws in Chechenya was ineffective because of the conflict between the union and the Russian governments, and it was a vivid example of the inability of the federal authorities to rely on measures of this kind in dealing with the economic crisis.

Of course Yeltsin could have tried to organize barter trade and somehow manage a barter economy. For instance, he could have tried to accumulate reserves of industrial goods that could be exchanged for grain in the countryside. This was exactly what the Russian government had tried to do in 1990 and 1991, but with very inefficient results. In 1917 Kerensky had tried the same policies, but also without success. It is just not possible under the circumstances to accumulate the necessary industrial resources in sufficient quantities to trade for foodstuffs and other basic commodities. Measures of this kind, therefore, were not going to be of any use. What then could be done?

Only one alternative remained, and that was to try to rapidly transform repressed inflation to open inflation, liberalize prices and the economy, introduce market mechanisms, and then, on the basis of these market mechanisms, try to resolve the basic crises of economic management. If the old-style economic regulations based on direct orders no longer worked, new mechanisms would have to be created as quickly as possible. What were the chances that these new mechanisms of economic management would work in practice? In analyzing the situation, it is clear that the odds were not at all good. Much more than liberalized prices are needed to get market mechanisms to work; a minimum requirement is some semblance of financial stability. Otherwise, immediately after prices are liberalized, there is a risk of finding yourself in the midst of hyperinflation, with money that is simply useless.

The possibility that price liberalization in Russia would immediately lapse into hyperinflation seemed very likely in the autumn of 1991. First, there were enormous financial imbalances. The budget deficit in the fourth quarter of 1991 was 20% of the country's GDP. It was very difficult to correctly estimate the monetary overhang accumulated during the years of financial disorder under Gorbachev, but it was certainly significant. In the presence of such enormous financial imbalances, it could be expected that an immediate reaction would be a drastic increase in the velocity of money, an uncontrollable increase in prices, runaway inflation, and the reappearance of shortages and distribution failures. For instance, if in November or December you tried to persuade anyone in Russia that within two months the enterprises would begin to worry about financial results, that they would really try to sell their products, or that it would be possible to buy goods with rubles, no one would have believed you; because it was truly felt that none of these things could ever happen.

It was understood in everyday economic life that many items could not be bought. State trade was institutionally structured in such a way that money was not important. There was a very strong tradition of the social stratification connected with access to resources that were in short supply. The man who had a friend in the shop—that is, the man who had a friend who had access to scarce resources—was an important member of society. He was called "the man at the corner." If you had money but no connections, you would not have access to goods in short supply. You were a nobody. Your money just demonstrated your lack of position in society. This was the economic reality not just for a year or two but for decades. One's grandparents were born into this society; they were accustomed to living all of their lives in accordance with this tradition. They were absolutely certain that it would continue, and there was no reason to believe that the newfangled ideas of the younger generation could change habits that had been formed over decades.

What we really feared most when we began the reforms was that after price liberalization, the stereotypical characteristics of the "shortage" economy would still prevail. Our concern was that even with liberalized prices, people would still not be in a position to buy anything with rubles due to very high inflation; and that, even though prices changed daily, people would continue to barter goods and not use money that was practically without value. If we hoped to change this attitude and introduce quite another form of economic regulation, we had to take radical steps to remove the greatest financial imbalances by imposing financial discipline on the enterprises and on the state. It was of course easier said than done.

We were happy in only one respect. After the August coup, the structures of political support linked to the different branches of the economy disappeared for a short time. The members of these structures were all strongly demoralized. For instance, Tysiakov, the leader of the military-industrial complex lobby, and Starodubtsev, the leader of the agricultural lobby—a lobby of the collective farms and state farms—who were both members of the state committee on the emergency situation, were now in prison. The Soviet army was practically nonexistent, and the Russian army was not yet in existence. We were in a very short-term situation in which the possibility of harsh and unpleasant measures was relatively high.

The only sensible thing was to exploit the opportunity as radically as we could by removing the financial imbalances. At this time, Russia had no normal central bank. There were sixteen central banks in the territory of the former Soviet Union, and in November the Gosbank of the Soviet Union had just issued its latest big credits to the union government. Each of the central banks of the republics issued credits to their governments without any coordination. It must be understood that it was impossible in a matter of a few weeks to introduce republican currencies into what had been a very integrated Soviet economy. Introducing a republican currency, especially in Russia, meant radically changing the mechanisms that linked its economy with those of the other republics. A lot of time is needed to prepare for this kind of reform; it cannot be completed in a matter of two or three months. You either negotiate a sensible common financial policy with the other republics, or you establish your own financial reforms and then see how they do. The choice, therefore, was to cooperate with the other republics or go it alone, urging the others to follow your example. We tried to negotiate joint reform programs with the republics, but the results were very disappointing. The economic and political situation in the republics was very strongly differentiated; their perspectives on economic transformation varied considerably, and no doubt some were seriously interested in continuing to receive the huge subsidies they were getting from Russia. We could, of course, agree on a joint monetary policy, but there was always the possibility that within two or three weeks we would hear from the president of the Ukraine that they were going to introduce their own reforms.

Thus we could either continue to discuss interminably a joint economic program or we could commence the transformation ourselves. One fact that indicated some hope for success was that Russia inherited about 65% of the former USSR's economic potential; and therefore any changes in Russia would create an enormous stimulus for change in the republics. So we decided to begin urging the other republics to radically liberalize their economies—especially through price liberalization—and to combine this price liberalization with very radical corrections of the financial imbalances.

First, we drastically reduced the amount of military spending. When we started our work in the government, I invited Barchuk to join us. He later became minister of finance in our government (he had previously been deputy minister of finance of the union government in charge of the budget). Barchuk was a long-term financial bureaucrat, very experienced in the Soviet Union Ministry of Finance and used to doing battle with the different branches of industry over the budget. I began discussing with him how to go about making a drastic improvement in the budget balance. He told me it was absolutely impossible. I said it was possible, and that the problem was not one of economic possibility but of political will. He said: "That's fine; try to cut military procurement by 30%." I decided not to cut it by 30%, but by 70%. I knew that it was a unique moment in history when such an act could be possible. Three months earlier, or four months later, it would have been considered unbelievable to even discuss the possibility of making such cuts in military expenditure. But the military-industrial lobby was demoralized at the time, and so we decided to cut expenditure on equipment very drastically.

I do not understand the arguments against our approach. They included: you should try to convert the military complex step-by-step; the military industry needs time to adapt to the new reality; you should have a long-term program; you should only cut the budget by 5%, etc. The military economy was the center of the economy, but if you adopted this approach, you would never convert the military industry. Gorbachev tried the step-by-step approach and it led nowhere. As long as the military industry believed it would get its orders, it could provide a thousand reasons why it was impossible to convert to civil production; for example, "It is of course necessary to convert, but why not build new production facilities with these additional billions and billions of rubles, and then we will discuss it?" Only when we drastically reduced the number of orders and, for instance, slashed tank production by thirty-eight times, or the amount of the armored personnel carriers by thirty-four times, did they accept the necessity of converting to civil production. So there were quite drastic reductions in the various military branches, especially those producing ordinary equipment (we had more tanks in our country than in the rest of the world put together and yet, in a time of serious crisis, we continued producing more tanks).

This made further adaptation possible. For instance, for years the military industry argued that it was absolutely impossible to start local production of oil and gas equipment. So enormous quantities had to be imported from the world market. Now, within a few months, our oil and gas production enterprises had begun receiving proposals from the military plants to start production of this type of equipment. A similar situation existed in the different branches of industry. The military enterprises, in fact, were usually able to adapt their production and find ways to replace the economic ties that were undermined by the dissolution of the Soviet Union. For instance, some Lithuanian enterprises stopped supplying spare parts for automobile production in Togliatti. Immediately, the military factories entered this market. The Ukrainian factories stopped producing motors for the enterprises in Altai and Krasnoyarsk. Once again, the military factories filled the void. Thus we created new technological resources that could be used to deal with the contraction of trade among the republics.

Our second drastic step was to cut subsidies. At the end of 1991 subsidies of consumer prices amounted to something like 15% of GDP. It was impossible to eliminate them entirely, but we hoped that we could reduce them by at least a half. This created serious, additional problems for industries that were used to getting subsidies, for example, our terribly inefficient agricultural producers. But it was the only option.

Another very difficult problem that had to be faced was tax reform. At the end of 1991 the old system of taxation was practically destroyed by the battle for property between the Russian and union governments. The union government tried to introduce a sales tax, which resembled a value-added tax, but its introduction was undermined by the decisions of the republican parliaments. We had two solutions to choose from: either use the existing turnover tax for a while or replace it by a value-added tax (which was more elastic in response to inflation) over the course of one or two years. We understood the dangers connected with a combination of drastic institutional reforms like price liberalization and drastic tax reform. We had also witnessed the experience of our friends in Poland who had to deal with the very difficult problems created by introducing a value-added tax after the reform process had started. However, we also knew that tax reform would be very difficult and unpopular further down the road. So we concluded that if you are going to be held accountable for all the unpleasant things that have to be done, you might as well combine them and get it over with all at once. Therefore, on 2 January 1992 we introduced a value-added tax at the rather high rate of 28%. The financial situation improved dramatically. The internal budget deficit was cut from 20% of GDP to something very near zero during the first few months of 1992.

At the time we were also able to change considerably the position and the policy of the central bank. The Central Bank of Russia was established during a period of disagreement between the Russian and union governments. It was created first of all for political purposes—to reinforce the position of the Russian government at a time when the union central bank was busily engaged in giving credits to the union government. In 1991 the Russian central bank was busy providing very cheap and enormous credits to Russian industries. So the entire ideology of this bank was an inflationary ideology—an ideology of cheap, popular credits and good relationships with industry. We were keen to convince the leaders of the central bank that the situation had changed dramatically and that they would now have to accept responsibility for the financial stability of Russia. This would require a new attitude toward reserve requirements, interest rates, and the amount of credit provided to the economy. The reserve requirements of commercial banks were increased from 5% in December 1991 to 20% on 1 April 1992. The basic interest rate was increased during 1992 step-by-step from 8% to 80% per annum, and the central bank generally kept money growth during the first half of 1992 to around 10% a month.

As a result of the combination of price liberalization and rather restrictive financial policy, during the first half of 1992 we could observe step-by-step the behavior of the various economic agents changing. I remember the first expression of change was sometime around 6 January, when angry producers stormed the White House asking "Where can we sell our cream?" It seemed nobody was buying cream in Moscow. To begin with, there was a lack of demand in the consumer goods market (especially for perishable goods) and later for goods produced for investment purposes (military goods, etc.). Gradually, problems of demand preoccupied Russian managers; not the usual problems of how to acquire resources in short supply, but the problem of how to sell the product and get paid for it.

This became very evident, for instance, in the changed position of the directors of the Russian building enterprise. The director of the building enterprise in a Russian city was once extremely powerful. The enterprise manager would have to get down on his knees just to get the director's signature on a piece of paper that suggested he might even consider a new building project. There were usually ten times more construction projects under way than was sensible to undertake, which explains why there are still so many projects under construction 20, 30, or 40 years later. In January and February there were strange sightings in various Russian cities of building enterprise directors running around in circles trying to find out who would order new projects from them, who could pay for the work, and who could provide the necessary financing to keep their enterprises alive.

Of course there was an enormous amount of cost-push inflation in the first few months. Under price liberalization, the enterprise director's first reaction was to increase prices steeply, regardless of the demand position or the obstacles connected with aggregate demand. The ordinary Russian enterprise director began by thinking he was in favor of price liberalization. Days later he was confronted with the fact that not only was he liberalizing his prices, but his supplier was showing him what price liberalization meant! In just a few months they would see both the real consequences and limitations of these measures. The combination of rather restrictive monetary policy and the strong cost-push inflation produced an enormous and very real crisis involving enterprise arrears.

This is a situation very familiar to all postcommunist economies. At the peak of the crisis in July 1992, the amount of arrears was approximately equivalent to two months' GDP. What made this process especially dangerous in Russia was the combination of the arrears crisis and the crisis of the payment mechanisms connected with the division of the single union ruble zone into the republican ruble zones. For example, in December 1991 it was quite possible in the

Ukraine to issue any amount of money and then conceal it in Russian territory. In January 1992 we were able to start introducing a mechanism that at least would provide us with some information about the monetary emissions from other republics to Russia. But we were receiving the information approximately four weeks late. So we tried to promote extremely restrictive policies. We cut down drastically on all of the state's financial expenditures including health care, education, and cultural projects. And salaries in the budgetary field were terribly low compared with those in business circles. At the same time, the republics had ample opportunity to issue new credits into Russian territory. Of course we understood the problem and tried as quickly as we could to prevent it from happening. But during the first half of the year all we had to show for our efforts were unpleasant consequences—the most unpleasant being the change in the payment mechanisms, which increased the time necessary for payments between Russian enterprises. The combination of delayed payments and the macroeconomic phenomena connected with the reduced rate of money growth resulted in an increase in the phenomenon of interenterprise arrears.

In July 1992 it seemed we were generally succeeding in tackling most of the serious problems that we faced at the beginning of the reform movement. We had minimum and maximum goals for our programs at the start of the reforms. The minimum was to convert repressed inflation to open inflation, create a basis on which market mechanisms could operate, preserve social stability, and establish a legal framework for the start of the privatization process. The maximum program was the minimum program plus the prevention of runaway inflation. In May or June it looked as if we were generally successful, even in the resolution of the maximum program. The inflation rate had been declining from month to month, and in July and August, on a monthly basis, it was about 10%. The economy was more or less liberalized; the behavior of the enterprises had changed drastically; shortages in the shops were practically eliminated; the economy was transformed from one of supply constraints to one of demand constraints; the enterprises' most serious worries were those concerning their customer's financial status; the budget was more or less in balance; and it appeared that we needed little else to succeed in our objectives of creating financial stability and the conditions necessary for the structural reform of our economy.

But this was only a very superficial picture of what was really happening. During May and June it had become increasingly obvious that it would be impossible to maintain these economic policies in the long term, not for economic reasons but for purely political ones. In January 1992, when the reform program was implemented, we created problems for the government—and for ourselves—in a wide range of sectors including: the military-industrial complex because of the radical cuts in military equipment; the agricultural lobby because of the cuts in subsidies; industry in general because of the increased level of taxation and generally restrictive monetary policy; the investment sector because of the drastic cuts in the demand for investment; and the budgetary field because of delays in payments from the budget and because salaries for the enterprises were slower in arriving than in the rest of the economy. So we undermined all the political bases needed to support the policies that we were trying to promote. For instance, branches of the economy that could not survive the cuts in subsidies and financial stabilization were interested in continued high inflation. Of course there were also healthy sectors of the economy that were genuinely interested in financial stability. In the Spring of 1992 the economy's large number of financial distortions paved the way for the creation of an alliance that included all of the enterprises, which was against continuing the restrictive monetary and budgetary policies. In May, when we were probably closer than ever to financial stabilization, the level of political support for the continuation of the reform process was the lowest it had been since the coup. The mass media and the public in general were quite certain that all of our problems were the result of too little money in the economy. All that was needed was more money. It was clear to them that only the monetarists in the government could not understand this, that is, those who were under the influence of the International Monetary Fund.

We were losing contact with all of the industrial structures. We could not even count any longer on unlimited support from the president, since he too was under a sea of pressure to correct this "silly" policy of financial stabilization. It was evident that the policy would have to be changed, leaving us with two options: either accept the change of economic policy and start maneuvering for new reforms or accept the change and resign immediately. These were the alternatives in June and July 1992.

We discussed the situation in great detail and decided to continue our efforts, even within this very much changed and unpleasant political framework, because of one very important factor. In the summer of 1992 we were about to embark on what was probably the biggest program of privatization in history. Preparations were at a crucial stage; the organizational structures were already in place, the necessary legislation and presidential decrees had been passed, and the privatization program had been approved by parliament. There was a real risk that a radical change in the direction of the reform movement could undermine the privatization program's chances of success, and thus the basis of a sensible economic policy. In hindsight, it was the correct decision. The reasons why are explained in the next chapter.

3   Privatization and Stabilization

As I have already said, many of the cleverer members of the communist elite were not at all dissatisfied that from 1991 onward total responsibility for the economy lay with the democrats. We had only one option remaining in the short time left at our disposal, and that was to create a social framework that would make a return to power by the communists if not impossible, at least not easy. We sensed that the population generally supported our economic reforms, but the social strata essential for the stability of a market economy and a capitalist society were missing. We had no entrepreneurs, no middle class, and no property ownership. Consequently, the development of the market economy was vulnerable to very sharp fluctuations in the country's political climate. Until this strata emerged, the future of Russia depended on the will of a popularly elected president who could not be expected to transform Russia single-handedly.

The principal task was privatizing the economy; a market economy could not function without the existence of private property. This task was especially difficult in Russia, probably more so than in the majority of other East European countries, because we had no tradition of legal private business. Private business existed in Hungary for at least twenty or twenty-five years before the beginning of the reform process. People there understood the procedures for raising money to transform a state enterprise into a private one. East Germany could look to West Germany for support. Eastern Europe's proximity to West European markets offered some possibility of success for their foreign-directed investments. In our case we had no legal private sector. If we decided to sell our enterprises to Russian entrepreneurs, the first question people would ask would be: "Where have they gotten their money?" After seventy years of strict prohibition, private enterprise was either connected to the black economy or was in the hands of the *nomenklatura*. Therefore the privatization process could not be based simply on the direct sale of assets of previously state-owned companies. Likewise, we could not rely on foreign capital alone because of the sheer size of the Russian economy. We were therefore faced with an enormous task. At the end of 1991 there were approximately 225,000 state enterprises to be privatized. During the previous two years of the reform process, around 150 had been privatized. This was the dimension of the task awaiting us.

In analyzing the situation, we realized that it would not be feasible to proceed on a case-by-case basis. Following this approach, each privatization would involve a unique procedure: the enterprise would have to be assessed and restructured. Then an attempt would be made to find potential investors and choose among them. All of this involves very difficult economic and legal procedures. Even the Germans, with their large reserves of qualified manpower and capital, had faced enormous difficulties in trying to privatize East Germany.

In our case it was quite clear that if we used a company-by-company approach, we would be privatizing the Russian economy well into the twenty-second century. Only a universal approach could be considered. Any other method would get us absolutely nowhere. It is possible of course to use the individual approach in a few specific cases: for instance, privatizing an airport or very large enterprise. But to get the whole process moving, a general approach must be adopted. Another reason for this was the enormous amount of corruption in the state system. A case-by-case approach would not increase efficiency and would give those in charge of operations a much greater opportunity to steal state property. Enterprise directors could create their own companies and then transfer state property to them. Such a system of property-ownership would not be regarded by the people as just and would risk political and social instability once more.

In adopting a universal approach, however, we somehow had to take into account the interests of the various social groups that had the power to block the implementation of the privatization procedures: for instance, the managers of the state enterprises, the working collectives, and the regional centers of power. Other groups, such as the military, the secret police, teachers, and medical workers, could also not be ignored without creating social conflict and ultimately making the whole program unsustainable.

It is impossible to devise an optimal strategy for privatization on purely economic grounds because the problem is not just economic; there are also long-term social and political implications. Nevertheless, to get going we had to decide on one principal program and structure it in such a way that it would be politically and socially sustainable. To maintain momentum we used the existing framework law on privatization, together with the special powers that had been granted to the president by the Congress of the

People's Deputies immediately after he assumed responsibility for economic policy. Otherwise it would have taken years to get the necessary legislation through parliament. This enabled us to start the process of small-scale privatization.

In Russia, with distances between regions of up to ten hours by plane, much time is needed to create the conditions necessary for large-scale privatization. An enormous number of detailed regulations are necessary. It was in this area that from early 1992 onward we have the best example of cooperation between Russian and foreign specialists; it was an example of the efficient use of technical assistance provided by the European Commission. By May/June 1992 we had more or less created the necessary conditions to start large-scale privatization of Russian industry. In June parliament adopted a new revised program of privatization, which included significant amendments that had the effect of creating long-term problems for us, such as the second privatization option in which 51% of an enterprise's shares could be bought by the working collective at a price only 1.7 times higher than the book value of the assets. Despite this setback, the program was in place and it was generally felt that we had managed to find the right balance among the different social groups. The regional governments had retained a certain amount of influence and the enterprise managers felt they had their possibilities as did the working collectives.

A presidential decree was issued in July 1992 while parliament was on vacation. Under a rule granted by the Congress of People's Deputies, if a decree is not opposed within two weeks it becomes law. So we were ready to begin the process of privatization. Unfortunately, it coincided with a civil crisis during which pressure mounted to weaken monetary policy and increase drastically the budget deficit. When we could no longer withstand the pressure, we loosened monetary and financial policy. At the same time, we hoped that it would not be too long before the large-scale privatization plan that we were about to put into effect would provide the social basis needed to straighten out our macroeconomic, financial, and monetary policies.

The social and political effects of privatization were felt from the beginning of September 1992. First, there was a noticeable change in the attitude of the enterprise directors. In the spring, the enterprises had combined forces against the government in their fight to secure easy credits. By autumn, a clear divide had begun to emerge between those who were still thinking of the splendid past—when their party committee gave them orders and provided the materials and money—and a younger, more energetic group who envisioned quite another future for themselves as managers of big private enterprises, in competition with other international private organizations and free to make their own decisions.

The change in attitude was very striking when seen at a personal level. For instance, I remember having discussions with a director of a very large military factory near Moscow. When we first met, he made it clear that he did not support us. He told me how much he liked the leaders of the military coup and that one of them was a close personal friend whom he supported. When we met again in September 1992, he was vociferous in his complaints about parliament not having yet passed the legislation to privatize his enterprise. There was great potential for obtaining Western orders for his product; and, as such, he strongly supported us against any attempt to interfere with the privatization process. By this time, the thought of a branch ministry telling him what to do had become unthinkable, and there were many cases like this among the industrial elite in Russia. Interestingly, the general population also took to the idea of privatization. Under our scheme we provided some privileges to the working collective, but we also distributed privatization"checks" to the general public, which the population could exchange directly for shares, or put into investment funds.

In mid-1992, before large-scale privatization began, when I visited a factory the working collective would confront me with questions such as: "Why are wages so low and prices so high? What will you do about unemployment?" In September/October, the questions were: "What should we do with our privatization checks? Is the scheme presented by our manager realistic?" Thus people were showing a lot of interest in the mechanics of privatization and asking many questions.

There was an obvious limit to how much we could achieve in a few months, but by the end of 1992 we had privatized 46,000 small enterprises. We then began privatizing the 5,000 biggest Russian enterprises by first converting them into joint stock companies and then selling the shares in these companies to the general public.

In January 1993, small-scale privatization slowed down, but we still managed to privatize approximately 2,000 small enterprises per month. Meanwhile, large-scale privatization gathered speed, especially after January when the preparations for conversion to joint stock companies was complete. This resulted in a huge increase in the number of people involved in the process of economic transformation who were actually working in the private sector.

The situation in the countryside was much more difficult than in the cities. For decades, the most socially active section of the population migrated to the big cities. So the remaining rural population were not at all enthusiastic about economic reforms in agriculture. It was difficult to get people to respond to any measures relating to the reforms. They had the impression that it was all a game, and that in a short time the communists would return and take their land back telling them it had all been a joke. People needed time to get used to the idea that this would not be the case. Nevertheless, we began introducing the idea of reforms to the countryside and developing the necessary legislation. There were many difficulties; for instance, there was a constitutional law, which we were not in position to change, that prohibited the resale of land for the first ten years except to local governments. This created enormous problems with mortgages and other credits to private agriculture. And, unfortunately, these problems could not be resolved easily, for example, by introducing a law relating to private property and land. Even so, we tried to set up a framework to promote change. First, all collective farms and state agricultural enterprises had to go through a process of registration requiring them to choose whether they wanted to keep their current status, that is, remain as collectives or state farms, be converted to joint stock companies or cooperatives, or be dissolved and converted to private farms. At the same time, we tried to reallocate surplus land or land that had been misused by the collective farms and state agricultural enterprises and redistribute it to those who wanted to begin private farming.

In 1992 practically all of the state farms and collectives had registered. Approximately one-third elected to keep the same form of management and two-thirds opted for change. We were also able to grant small plots of land to nearly every Russian citizen who wanted one. (The figure is very modest, something like 6% of the total.) In Russia, where the majority of the urban population is only one or two generations removed from farming, there is an eagerness to engage in small agricultural production outside of the cities. During communist rule it had been very difficult to obtain these plots of land, but now we were able to double the number available and offer one to practically everybody. The effects of these changes became apparent in the spring of 1993; when many regions of Russia experienced low market demand for potatoes and other vegetables, because the production of private plots had increased to the extent that the majority of people were now able to feed themselves.

In mid-1993 we have something like 250,000 private farms in Russia, averaging thirty-three hectares each. The number is expanding by approximately 10,000 new farms a month. There is a long way to go, because the output of the private sector amounts to a very small percentage, say 6–8%, of total agricultural output. But it is a rapidly increasing and important sector and provides additional social and political support for the reforms. In the future, when the directors of the old-style collectives complain that conditions are very bad and consequently productivity is very low, they will be confronted not by the government but by agricultural workers, who will say that bad management is to blame. Then the workers will press for a change to a different, more efficient way of farming. In the past it was difficult to persuade farmers to take reform seriously. Now it would be hard to convince them to think otherwise. The situation is almost irreversible; people would fight to keep their land.

Even in days of communism, when private plots made up a very small percentage of the collective farm, they produced something like 28% of the meat and 50% of the potatoes. What has happened in the last year is that the collective sector has become smaller and smaller, and the private plots bigger and bigger. Livestock is also being transferred from the collectives to individuals. Reports in the Russian press, even in the international press, attributed the big drop in the amount of livestock held by the state farms and collectives to a shortage of grain and feed. The results of investigations offered quite another picture. The livestock was being redistributed from collectives to private hands. Even now, although we are only in the initial stages of the agricultural transformation, private farmers and private plots produced approximately 34% of agricultural products from as little as 12–13% of the arable land. But despite this progress, the transformation in the countryside is proceeding slowly and is not without serious political problems.

The loosening of financial policy led to an increased budget deficit, additional expenditure, and cheap credits and created a new political atmosphere. Those who tried to defend these policies maintained that if the enterprises were given cheap money, it would not create additional inflation—on the grounds that inflation in our country was cost-push, not demand-pull. Therefore the result would be increased productivity. Within two months the consequences of these policies were plain to see. In August 1992 inflation was 9–10%, due to the tight monetary policy of the previous months. After the monetary explosion in June, July, and August, during which money supply growth increased from 10% to 25%, monthly rates of inflation jumped from 10% in August to 25% in September, October, and November.

These results were so bad that they undermined the prevailing political consensus that favored hyperinflationary policies. Even by September it had become possible for the government to return to a more restrictive financial policy. We immediately cut the budget deficit drastically so that the budget was practically balanced from September to December. This created a basis for slowing down the rate of money increase.

But the central bank continued to be rather aggressive with monetary policy. In September it issued enormous additional credits, including credits to the commonwealth states. By October and November it was obvious even to the central bank that this hyperinflationary policy was not producing politically acceptable results. In October the central bank lowered the amount of credit available to commercial banks, and in November we were able to drastically reduce the rate of increase of the monetary supply—cutting, for instance, the monthly rates from 32% in September to 6% in November. This also reversed the situation that had developed with regard to the exchange rate. At the beginning of 1992, as a result of our restrictive monetary policy, we were able to cut the nominal dollar/ruble exchange rate from 230 rubles per dollar in January 1992 to something like 115 rubles in June. Until May the rate was based on general macroeconomic fundamentals. In June, when the macroeconomic situation worsened, the low price of the dollar was connected with excessive intervention by the central bank in the currency market. From July onward there was a very rapid fall in the external value of the ruble, closely connected with the enormous credit expansion during July, August, and September. The ruble fell from 115 rubles per dollar in June 1992 to 440 rubles in the middle of November. At that point, an improvement in the macroeconomic situation and a reduction in the increase in the money supply created the conditions necessary for once more stabilizing the ruble/dollar exchange rate. It dropped from 450 rubles in mid-November to 398 on December 8, the last day of our government's work.

Thus by November there was no longer a strong pro-inflation coalition. Also, as the structural changes had affected people in all areas—economic, political, and social—we were again able to adopt sensible, restrictive monetary and financial policies and promote the case for stabilization. During the Seventh Congress of the People's Deputies, however, personnel changes in the government became inevitable. Someone had to pay the consequences for the serious social costs connected with transforming the economy. But the continuation of sensible policies was no longer strongly dependent on personalities.

Those who supported a change in the government's leadership hoped very much that such a change would immediately lead to radical changes in economic policymaking. Since most governments are somewhat divided and there are often many sources of influence and differing views about economic policy, it was not surprising that immediately after the change in the government there was an attempt to change the essence of economic policy. In its first ten days, the new government issued an enormous amount of cheap credits and greatly increased the state budget deficit. It tried to freeze the price of basic industrial and consumer commodities, and it adopted a resolution to stop, at least temporarily, privatization of the biggest military enterprises.

But the situation was different now, and these measures did not receive a lot of popular support. The immediate result was a rapid acceleration of inflation. Weekly inflation jumped from approximately 5% in the middle of December to 7–8% in the last two weeks of December and the first two weeks of January 1993. For the first time in months consumer goods were no longer readily available. Shortages reappeared in Moscow. There was a very serious danger of hyperinflation and this, together with the worsening situation in the consumer goods market, was understood by the people to be closely related to recent government policies.

Thus, by the middle of January the government was once more under the influence of the reform group. It abandoned its decision to liberalize prices and stated once more that anti-inflationary policies were the top priority. It tried to cut back on the state expenditure and became involved in a dispute with the central bank over the growth of the money supply, interest rates, and so on. The attempt to stop privatization of the biggest military-industrial enterprises was opposed not by a small pro-presidential faction in parliament or a few liberals, but by the enterprise directors and the working collectives themselves. They said: "You cannot provide us with military orders, nor is there any guarantee that you will buy our products. Therefore give us our freedom. We are negotiating our own orders from the West, so please go away."

The reform process was no longer dependent on the political will or economic logic of a few people. A social base was being created from which came support for the reforms. From my point of view, this is why we won on the second question in the April 1993 referendum—that is, the question on support for the government's economic policy. This result must have been difficult for a foreign observer to understand, and in truth it is difficult even for me. I never expected that we would win on this question, and now I am in the position of Henry V who had to explain how he won the Battle of Agincourt! It is obvious that we underestimated how much life really had changed in the average Russian city during the previous year and a half. Of course, prices are high and there are enormous problems with corruption and instability. There is also the prospect of serious unemployment, which we have not had to face until now. But in everyday life the improvements are obvious. People no longer have to go to Moscow each week to buy basic foodstuffs, travelling sometimes up to 1,000 kilometers—quite a normal practice for Russians because food could not be bought anywhere else. Now people in the cities don't have to wait in line for hours to get bread, milk, or meat. They can buy foods they never dreamed of seeing in their own city. And they don't need to wait years before they are in a position to get them.

It is also possible to earn money without restrictions. In the past, it was a big problem for the young, intelligent, and active to earn money because it was prohibited. Now if you are young and have even a little energy, you can somehow manage. There are opportunities in this enormous economy that were previously nonexistent. Take, for example, the big apartments in the center of the big cities, especially Moscow and St. Petersburg, where many lived in communal flats shared by more than one family. It must have seemed to people living in those apartments that they would be there forever, that no rehousing programs could ever solve their problems, that even after waiting in line for fifteen or twenty years they would get nothing. When the housing market was introduced, it became obvious that these huge apartments in the center of Moscow and St. Petersburg were very valuable. They could be refurbished and rented out to foreign firms or commercial banks for enormous sums of money, certainly enormous in view of people earning a salary the equivalent of $30 per month. So people are moving into individual apartments, while the buildings in the center are being developed. In Moscow this kind of project represents about 20% of new construction, and it helps finance the construction of housing projects for ordinary citizens.

I am not saying that the situation is perfect, but neither is it a story of complete misery. It is a rapidly changing world, a world of opportunities—not just at the governmental level but at the level of the ordinary citizen. If people today were asked if they would like to go back to the days of cheap, dreadful salami for which you had to travel 1,000 kilometers and then wait three hours in line, they would say no.

Success in the referendum, especially on the second question, has created enormous opportunities for the government and the president. It is clear that the attempts of parliament and the procommunist regional soviets to stop the privatization process will not succeed. This provides new impetus to speeding up the transformation process. The most difficult problem is assuring financial stability. The general preconditions for a sensible financial policy exist. The system of tax collection is not bad. But during political campaigns and times of political confrontation, there is a temptation to buy support. Competing centers of power, particularly those of the president and parliament, present many dangers for the continuation of a stable financial policy in Russia. Even when there are signs of financial stabilization and the inflation figures have improved, it does not mean that the danger or the threat of an explosion in inflation has been removed. Even weekly inflation of 3% is very dangerous. Combined with political upheaval, it could rapidly lead to unsustainable high inflation or even hyperinflation, with terrible consequences for the future of the market economy and the evolution of democratic institutions in Russia. This is a very serious concern. So, even with the prospect of many political problems to come, a strict financial policy is still the only one worth pursuing, because it is the only one that can produce long-term sustainable results.

Over the next few years Russia will be confronted with many difficult economic problems. Reductions in the rate of inflation will inevitably bring up the level of unemployment, which is now only a little more than 1% of the labor force. The process of structural transformation will lead to the beginning of really serious financial difficulties—even bankruptcy—for some of the big enterprises. Privatization may help them raise more cash, but it will take time to establish clear property rights, strong institutional owners, and so on. There will also be problems connected with the low level of national savings due to the serious problems of the state budget and the well-established habits of Russian households. In the days of communism, when the situation was stable, personal savings in Russia was around 2% of GDP. A private economy cannot be developed on this level of savings. But savings rates are very difficult to change using political measures. They will be changed by time and a general improvement in the level of people's welfare, not by simply changing economic instruments.

If there are many difficulties ahead, there are also enormous opportunities. Russia probably has the cheapest and most qualified labor force in the world. It is generally much more qualified than that of, for instance, Southeast Asia, and it is much cheaper now. It is a country with long-term cheap energy and enormous investment possibilities.

If we can maintain political stability, I am sure that by the beginning of the twenty-first century Russia, although still poor, will be one of the most dynamically developing countries in the world. I will not deny that investment in the Russian economy involves a risk, even though the referendum assures us of the support of the president and the people. But for big companies, not investing also involves a risk—the risk of being left behind when everybody else is already in the market. It would not do to be left outside such a market.

If I were asked what was the most serious danger facing Russia today, I would probably say the danger of the Weimar syndrome. In the other young democracies the difficult problems of economic transformation have been mitigated by a new sense of national pride—in Czechoslovakia, Poland, and the Baltic states, for instance. A certain amount of suffering is bearable under the circumstances. This is not so in Russia. In addition to their economic suffering, Russia has lost an empire. It would be very easy to exploit the sense of loss and economic hardship to create an aggressive national movement, using slogans such as, "We have not been defeated in the war; rather we have been betrayed and the traitors are in power and are selling our country to the foreigners." This strategy could succeed if the Russian economy became stagnant during the next few years, like the German economy after World War I. This would be a very dangerous situation for world order. Luckily in Russia, social, political, and economic developments have so far shown that this outcome is not at all inevitable. If we remain strong and united, and if the West's policies toward Russia and the Russian government's policies toward the West are based on common sense, success will be ours.

International
Monetary Policy:
A Personal View

Karl Otto Pöhl

1

International Cooperation in Monetary Policy and Currency Management

I

It's an honor and a pleasure for me to be invited to present the Lionel Robbins lecture. I have to say right at the beginning, however, that I am not an academician or a professional economist, but a businessman and a banker. So don't expect the systematic analysis you would normally get from an academic lecture at the London School of Economics, but rather an eclectic, sometimes anecdotal report about some of my experiences in more than twenty years on the international monetary stage, first as state secretary for national and international monetary policy in the German finance ministry, and later as vice-president and then president of the Bundesbank. In different capacities I have not only witnessed but also participated in nearly all important events related to international monetary decisionmaking. So what I'm saying comes from the horse's mouth, which may provide a certain compensation for the fact that my report is not at all complete or objective.

I will first talk about international cooperation in the G-5 and later the G-7, particularly the efforts to stabilize exchange rates after the breakdown of the Bretton Woods system (BWS). I will then deal with the issue of monetary integration in Europe, which did not start with Maastricht or with the European monetary system (EMS) but in 1973, which may be the most important year in postwar history as far as monetary policy is concerned. I believe it may be appropriate to elaborate a little on the historical background of some recent problems.

II

I want to start with a brief description of the institutional position of the Bundesbank in the German political system and its basic philosophy, which one has to comprehend if one wants to understand the policy of the Bundesbank and its behavior in the process of international cooperation, both within the G-7 and vis-à-vis European monetary arrangements (first the so-called snake and then the EMS).

The Bundesbank was established only in 1957. Its predecessor was the Bank Deutscher Länder, which consisted of ten, then eleven, central banks of the German Länder, which together with the board (Direktorium) formed the central bank council, a decentralized, federalistic central bank system. This model, by the way, was used when the committee of the EC central bank governors (under my chairmanship) drafted the text for a statute of a European central bank, which became part of the Maastricht Treaty.

Once the Bundesbank was established, its decentralized character was maintained until today. After the unification of Germany, however, the principle of "one state, one central bank" was slightly changed. Today Germany consists of sixteen Länder but only nine Landeszentralbanken (LZB). (Before I resigned as president of the Bundesbank, I had proposed that there be seven instead of nine.) The presidents of the Landeszentralbanken are appointed by the second chamber, the Bundesrat (i.e., the Länder).

The president of the Bundesbank and the chairman of the central bank council and the executive board are appointed by the Bundespräsident on the proposal of the federal government, like the presidents of the LZBs, normally for a tenure of eight years. (There is an ongoing discussion in the United States concerning whether federal reserve presidents should be appointed by politicians or bankers.) Together they form the central bank council, which is the decisionmaking body. It meets every two weeks under the chairmanship of the president of the Bundesbank. Every member, including the chairman, has one vote.

The members of the central bank council have different social, political, and professional backgrounds. Only a few have made their career in the central bank or in banking. Some are former politicians, mainly state finance ministers, and some are former civil servants, like the current president and myself. Others have an academic background. The rather complicated structure of the central bank council was designed by lawmakers in 1957 to assure the independence of the Bundesbank, which is the main reason for its unique position in the German political system and its power in international monetary policy as well. The members of the central bank council are not accountable for their decisions to the federal government or to state governments or parliaments, and they are not subject to instructions by those institutions. Their far-reaching independence was not undisputed when the Bundesbank law was written. Konrad Adenauer, for instance, was clearly against it and wanted the central bank to be closer to the government as it is in most countries. But finally the advocates of independence succeeded—among them Ludwig Erhard, the father of the German economic miracle, as it was called.

Three main reasons for Bundesbank independence can be mentioned: First, there is deep public suspicion of a strong central government, in reaction to the overcentralization of the Nazi regime. We find this in other areas of German politics as well: strong states, strong unions, self-government of the different branches of the social security system, regional diversification of government agencies, etc. Germany is in many respects a country without a center. The second reason: The prevailing economic and social theory after the war was neoliberalism, which had been formulated by Austrian-German authors like Hayek, Eucken, Röpke, and Müller-Armack, and which had been transformed under the name *soziale Marktwirtschaft* into economic policy with overwhelming success by Ludwig Erhard. Sound money is part of the framework *(Rahmenbedingungen)* for functioning markets and social justice *(soziale Gerechtigkeit)*.

The third reason is by far the most important: The German people had experienced the destruction of their currency twice in recent history, once during the hyperinflation after World War I and then again after World War II. When inflation reached its peak in 1923, $1 was worth 4.2 trillion Reichsmark. Inflation destroyed the economic base of the middle class and was one of the main reasons for the failure of the Weimar Republic. By coincidence, 1923 was also the year of the Hitler putsch in Munich—the first appearance of the Nazis on the political stage. This is why in the 1950s Germany's lawmakers believed that inflation should never be allowed in their country again, and an independent central bank would be the best way to assure this.

III

The main task of the Bundesbank is to maintain price stability; at least this is the Bundesbank's understanding of its role. It's widely accepted in Germany and strongly supported by public opinion, which is by far the strongest ally of the Bundesbank. "Not everybody believes in God, but everybody believes in the Bundesbank," as Jacques Delors once said. With respect to price stability, the Bundesbank law is rather vague. It says: The task of the Bundesbank is "to safeguard the currency," *(die Währung zu sichern)*. This could—and in the understanding of the lawmaker does—include the internal and external value of the currency. Both are of course closely related. Over time external stability, (exchange-rate stability) became increasingly incompatible with internal stability (price stability). Indeed, there is a major conflict between the commitment to the Bretton Woods agreement and several later international agreements (like the Louvre agreement and, last but not least, the EMS) to defend fixed exchange rates and to maintain domestic price stability.

This conflict has been a central theme in the history of German monetary policy making since the late 1960s and it is the main focus of my lecture. The Bundesbank always decided in favor of domestic price stability and sacrificed exchange-rate stability if necessary. There are many statements by Bundesbank officials (including myself when I was president) that the majority of the central bank council members felt responsible for price stability in Germany but not, for instance, for a certain exchange rate of the dollar (or as it was even suggested on some occasions, of the yen). Finally, the Bundesbank did not even feel responsible for the EMS. This position was emphasized very recently by the new president of the Bundesbank, Hans Tietmeyer, when he said that, "The Bundesbank cannot be the Central Bank of Europe." So we also experienced continuity in this respect.

The conflict between domestic monetary necessities and a commitment to defend a certain exchange rate is of course not unique to Germany. But in most countries, central banks had to raise interest rates and tighten monetary policy; that is, they pursued a rather deflationary policy in order to defend exchange rates regarded as unsustainable by the currency markets. We still remember recent examples.

For the Bundesbank it was mostly the other way around. The markets expected an appreciation of the deutsche mark in terms of the dollar and/or European currencies. This caused an inflow of money and capital that threatened to destroy the framework of monetary discipline in Germany. In fact, since 1969 the deutsche mark has appreciated against the dollar (before the revaluation) by 137%, against the French franc by 180%, and against the British pound by 319%. (See figure 4.1.)

One reason for the development of the external value of the deutsche mark was the better consumer price performance in Germany than in most other industrialized countries. (German inflation has averaged 3.3% since 1960.) (See figure 4.2.)

In fact, Germany was the only OECD country in the 1970s, after the oil crisis that never experienced a double-digit inflation rate. Whereas even countries like Switzerland and Japan sometimes had inflation of over 20% during that period.

I am particularly proud that inflation remained below 3% for eight of the eleven and one-half years that I was president of the Bundesbank. When I took office in 1980 inflation was above 7%, and when I resigned in 1991 it was above 4%—a consequence of German unification—but still much lower than market expectations. On balance, the record of the Bundesbank as far as inflation is concerned has been pretty good.

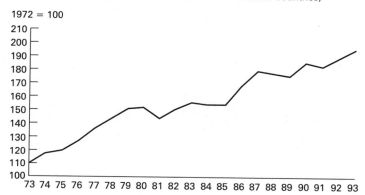

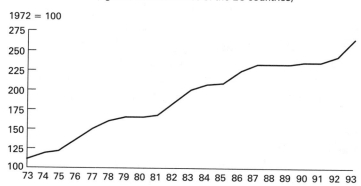

Figure 4.1
Nominal external value of the deutsche mark

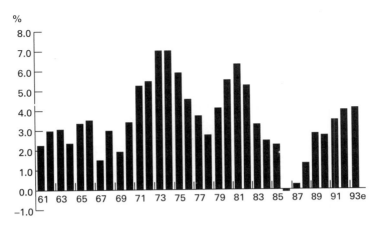

Figure 4.2
Inflation rates: West Germany

Figure 4.3 shows that, due to the considerably lower German inflation rate the deutsche mark, in spite of strong nominal appreciation, was almost stable in real terms against all major currencies (basket of eighteen currencies). Consequently, the competitiveness of the German economy was maintained in spite of revaluation. This can be seen as a result of the consequent anti-inflationary policy of the Bundesbank. Nevertheless, it is obvious that exchange-rate turbulence has not made monetary policy easier. An indication of this is the development of money supply figures. In fact, the Bundesbank was the first central bank to publish money supply targets. But I must admit that the targets have missed their mark several times since they have been published, most of the time for external reasons. (See figure 4.4.)

I do not want to discuss whether money supply targets are still a reliable compass. With enormous volatility in foreign exchange markets and the emergence of sophisticated

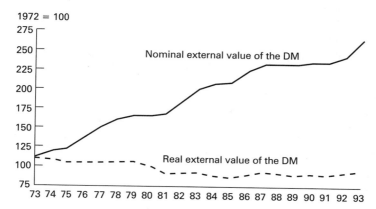

Figure 4.3
Gap between nominal external value and real external value of the deutsche mark

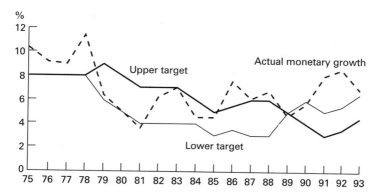

Figure 4.4
Monetary targets and actual developments
Note: In 1988 the Bundesbank switched from so-called central bank money to money stock M3 as its reference indicator.

new instruments in financial markets, it's hard to find any indicator of consistent accuracy. Therefore I think it is fair to say that money supply figures should only be used with caution and that other indicators should be taken into account as well before decisions are made.

Nevertheless, money matters; if a central bank realizes that money supply figures are exploding, it should be taken as a clear signal that inflation is around the corner. There are too many examples—not the least in this country—where this signal was ignored, and the results are well known.

IV

The reason why the Bundesbank very often had to defend exchange rates by intervening or sometimes even by hesitating to implement decisions that the central bank council considered necessary is very simple: The independence of the Bundesbank is not unlimited. Legally it is limited by the fact that the government, not the Bundesbank, is ultimately responsible for exchange-rate arrangements with other governments. Actually there is no law in Germany where this is prescribed, but it has never been disputed, not even by the Bundesbank. It followed legally from the Bretton Woods treaty, which was of course an international treaty among governments.

This rule was adopted when the EMS was founded in spite of the fact that the EMS is based on an agreement among central banks, especially the intervention obligations, credit facilities, and settlement procedures. During the negotiations of the Basel/Nyborg agreement (12/13 September 1987), I suggested that the decision to change exchange rates in the EMS should be put in the hands of the committee of European Community Central bank governors in order to depoliticize these decisions and to allow the system more flexibility. But this suggestion was bluntly rejected by all governments, including Germany's, which is very regrettable because it has become obvious that governments very often are unable to agree on a convincing realignment of exchange rates in a timely fashion. The last time we witnessed this was in 1992. This certainly has been one of the reasons for the de facto collapse of the EMS. One should not blame unknown or even known speculators but rather the governments who are responsible for exchange-rate changes according to the EMS rules. The Bundesbank, I assume, is much happier living with a de facto floating system, with practically no intervention obligations for the time being, than with a system of fixed but adjustable exchange rates, which Allen Walters accurately called "half-baked" because adjustments never take place at the right moment.

V

I will talk about the EMS and the problems of a monetary union in Europe. But now I would like to elaborate on international cooperation in terms of monetary policy making, an area in which I have participated in different capacities for more than twenty years. When I became state secretary for national and international monetary policy in the German finance ministry following the 1972 elections, Helmut Schmidt was finance minister. Valery Giscard d'Estaing was finance minister of France and George Schultz was Treasury Secretary of the United States—a distinguished group of people indeed. In my view, this is not without relevance because I wonder what would have happened to the world during those turbulent times without the strong leadership and cooperation of these three people in particular (i.e., Schmidt, Giscard, and Schultz). Remember: It was the time of the collapse of the Bretton Woods system and the first oil crisis. The year 1973 also marked the beginning of both G-5 (G-7) cooperation and the first attempt to create a European system at fixed (but adjustable) exchange rates. The G-5, actually, was casually founded in May 1973 on a Sunday afternoon when George Schultz had invited Valery Giscard d'Estaing, Helmut Schmidt, and Tony Barber, the British chancellor, for an informal talk in the library of the White House. The meeting was also attended by Paul Volcker, then undersecretary for monetary affairs in the United States, Claude Pierre Brossolet, directeur général of the French treasury, Derek Mitchell, permanent secretary of the British treasury, and myself. After the dust of the currency crisis had settled, the tone of the discussions became less confrontational. In fact, those in the meeting who had not known each other before began to like each other. At least they recognized that the Western world was in a deep crisis (the possibility of an oil crisis had already been mentioned in that first meeting) and that their leadership was extremely important. I cannot remember who made the proposal, but finally the group agreed to hold regular meetings, and Helmut Schmidt suggested calling it the library group. Our next meeting took place at Camp David and another was held in Tours (France). Later, the Japanese were invited to participate as were the central bank governors. The preparatory and operational work was done more and more by the finance ministers' deputies, a group that remains one of the most efficient in this area. The library group was also the nucleus of the summit meetings of the heads of state and governments, which from the beginning included Italy and Canada (G-7). Only in 1987 did the finance ministers and central bank governors reluctantly accept an enlargement of the G-5 under pressure from the G-5 heads of governments.)

VI

From the German point of view, the decision to free the Bundesbank from its obligation under the IMF rules to purchase any amount of dollars offered by the foreign exchange markets, which ultimately led to the floating of the deutsche mark, was the most important event in monetary history since the currency reform of 1948. It was of course also the end of the system of fixed exchange rates that had served the world well. But March 1973 was only the last act of a long drama. As a result of lax monetary and fiscal policy and inflationary financing of the Vietnam War, the dollar as the anchor currency of the system lost confidence. The deutsche mark (and the Swiss franc) were increasingly regarded as alternatives because they were hard currencies, fully convertible, and with no restrictions on capital movements.

But the effect of capital inflows that had to be financed by the Bundesbank meant an increase in liquidity, which could not easily be neutralized with the instruments available at that time. (Later the Bundesbank developed repurchase agreements, which made it much easier to deal with such huge capital movements.) In 1968 the Bundesbank had urged the government to revalue the deutsche mark in order to regain room to maneuver. But opinion was split within the coalition government. The Social Democrats—in particular their economic minister, Karl Schiller, who had succeeded Ludwig Erhard and had become almost as popular—were in favor of revaluation. The Christian Democratic Union (CDU) together with most of big business and leading bankers were against it. So this rather complex issue became the main subject of the election campaign. Schiller succeeded, and for the first time in postwar history the Social Democrats could form a coalition government with the Liberals as junior partners under Chancellor Willy Brandt. Money does matter.

Finally, in 1969 the deutsche mark was appreciated against the dollar and to the same degree against the French franc and the British pound. But this did not calm the markets for long. On the contrary, the revaluation strengthened the deutsche mark and made it even more attractive for capital investments. So the government tried to reduce the growing upward pressure on the mark by introducing capital control measures, which were in stark contrast to the liberal German economic policy; but ultimately they didn't work. (Those today who advocate capital controls to fight speculators should study that experience.) Even Switzerland at some point introduced negative interest rates on the Swiss franc deposits to discourage capital inflows.

Neither the "Bardepot" nor other divestible measures could stop the capital inflows, which of course were the result of the dwindling confidence in the U.S. dollar. The United States at the time maintained an attitude of benign neglect; it was not ready to subordinate its internal monetary and fiscal policy in defense of the fixed exchange-rate system. United States Treasury Secretary John Connally put it quite bluntly: "It's our currency but it's your problem."

Germany was the main target of the capital move out of the dollar. From the beginning of 1970 to May 1971 the currency reserves of the Bundesbank increased from 20 billion to 69 billion deutsche marks. A new reserve currency was born. (See figure 4.5.) But at the same time monetary policy lost its grip and inflation began an alarming rise.

So in May 1971, Karl Schiller made the lonely decision to let the deutsche mark float (technically allowing the Bundesbank not to intervene any more). The reaction outside of Germany was disastrous. I remember there was a meeting

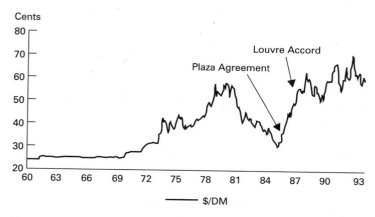

Figure 4.5
Rising value of the deutsche mark against the dollar over the last thirty years

of the chairmen of the leading commercial bankers of the world (International Monetary Conference, or IMC) in Munich that was attended by Connally but not Schiller, who did not even meet with Connally at this occasion, where Connally made some very rude remarks about German exchange rate policies.

VII

With the floating of the deutsche mark in 1971 the Bretton Woods system started to erode. The next pillar crumbled in August 1971 when President Richard Nixon closed the "gold window;" that is, the United States cancelled its commitment to convert the dollar into gold at any time at a fixed price ($38 an ounce). Actually this gold guarantee of the dollar already existed only on paper. Under heavy political pressure Germany decided not to take advantage of the gold rule of the Bretton Woods agreement ("blessing brief").

The IMF members tried one last time to fix the exchange-rate system through the famous Smithsonian agreement. Nixon called it "the most important exchange rate agreement in world history after World War II." But it lasted only a few weeks. One currency crisis followed another. In February 1973 the dollar was devalued again. However, it was too late; defending fixed exchange rates was not credible anymore. In March 1973 the Bretton Woods system collapsed, and the fate of currencies was left to the markets. A legendary era had come to an end.

The majority of the Bundesbank council was not unhappy with this result (except its president, Karl Klasen, who had always been an advocate of fixed exchange rates). Monetary policy under the fixed exchange-rate system had become a nightmare. Inflation had risen to 7%, which was absolutely unacceptable in Germany; and the money supply increased 28% between December 1972 and March 1973.

VIII

The now possible free floating gave the Bundesbank the opportunity to raise its minimum reserve requirements. It took advantage of this opportunity the same day that the central banks were released from the intervention obligation by raising the minimum reserve requirements to 15%. The government supported the restrictive policy of the Bundesbank using the instruments of the law of stability and growth *(Stabilitäts- und Wachstumsgesetz).* An 11% tax on investments, additional income taxation, and a huge issuance of government bonds were part of the consolidation program. The amount of 1.5 billion deutsche marks raised from the bond placement was retained in a special account at the Bundesbank, effectively withdrawing it from circulation.

As soon as the success of this tight monetary and fiscal policy was evident, the world was hit by another shock, the oil crisis. At least at this stage the system of fixed exchange rates would have finally broken down. The now implemented floating system proved to be extraordinarily useful. The government very quickly gave up its restrictive fiscal policy because it feared the negative impact of the oil crisis on economic growth. At the same time, the Bundesbank stuck to its restrictive course. The Bundesbank's tight monetary policy was contrary to the prevailing international consensus that the accelerating oil prices would have a deflationary impact on the economy. The majority of countries therefore followed a monetary policy that attempted to fight anticipated deflation; the results in 1974 and 1975 were devastating. Japan, for example, experienced inflation rates of 25%. (In 1974 the inflation rate in England was 16%, and in 1975 24.2%.) In contrast, Germany was quite successful in avoiding inflation despite homemade problems such as wage increases, which totally ignored the external inflationary environment. Under the protection of flexible exchange rates, the Bundesbank managed to escape the international inflationary spiral.

Germany, as I have already mentioned, was the only OECD country that managed to avoid double-digit inflation rates. In the period from 1973 to 1979 consumer prices rose 39%, whereas during the same period the consumer price index (CPI) in the United States rose by 87% and in the average OECD countries by 110%. In 1978 Germany was very close to achieving its goal of price stability in combination with high employment. The inflation rate at the time was only 2.7%. The financial markets rewarded this success by regarding the deutsche mark more and more as an alternative to the U.S. dollar. As a result of the political and economic weakness of the United States, the dollar experienced a deep crisis. At the same time, the external value of the deutsche mark rose so quickly that the competitiveness of the German economy faced increasing danger. First, its current account surplus rose to record high levels. As a consequence, German monetary policy was heavily criticized, and its leaders were put under international pressure to do more for international economic growth. At the Bonn summit meeting in 1978, this criticism led to the evolution of the locomotive theory, the essence of which was that surplus countries should pull the world out of the recession by implementing more expansionary fiscal and monetary policies.

IX

At the time the Bundesbank was in the midst of a severe dilemma. As I mentioned earlier, the Bundesbank in 1974 was the first central bank in the world to publish a monetary target. It had therewith published a quantitative target, which gave everybody the opportunity to clearly read the success or failure of its monetary policy. For 1978 the monetary target was defined at 8%. The actual monetary expansion was 11.4%, which was far more than the target. Under normal circumstances this overshooting of monetary growth would have led to the adoption of a restrictive monetary policy by the Bundesbank. High budget deficits and a cost-increasing wage policy pointed in the same direction. The possibility of an even more restrictive monetary policy was discussed intensively in the central bank council, but the fear of a further appreciation of the deutsche mark led the council to hesitate. The significant overshooting was regarded as the lesser evil; however, this proved to be false.

This is why the course of monetary policy had to be more restrictive in the beginning of the 1980s. The decline of the dollar (in terms of the deutsche mark), which already had begun in 1968 and had accelerated in 1973, reached a dramatic climax in 1979 at the time of the IMF/World Bank meeting in Belgrad. At the time the Carter administration was strongly advocating international cooperation; U.S. policy was expansionary and finally inflationary, which drove the dollar into a dramatic tailspin. (See figure 4.6.)

On its way to Belgrade, the American delegation made a stopover in Hamburg, at the private home of Chancellor Helmut Schmidt. The delegation urged Otmar Emminger, the president of the Bundesbank, and me to intervene in the exchange markets in a strong and coordinated way to sta-

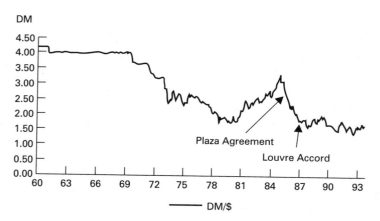

Figure 4.6
Volatility in exchange rates after free floating

bilize the dollar. Schmidt and Emminger bluntly refused because inflation in Germany was on the rise, and we were convinced that, given the U.S. policy, intervention was not credible in the markets. Emminger and I continued the discussions in Belgrade with Paul Volcker, who had just been appointed chairman of the Fed. Volcker left the IMF meeting before it was over, returned to the United States, and did the only thing that promised change: he raised interest rates dramatically.

When Ronald Reagan became president of the United States in 1981, a new team (including Donald Regan and Beryl Sprinkle, a follower of the Friedman school in Chicago) took over at the U.S. Treasury. So for years, intervention in exchange markets and efforts to stabilize the exchange rate of the dollar were not on the agenda. The Bundesbank advocated a more pragmatic view. We thought that interventions should not entirely be excluded from the set of instruments of monetary policy, but we basically agreed with the U.S. Treasury that external monetary stability could only be achieved in the end by domestic monetary discipline, that is, each country was responsible for putting its own house in order.

X

This did not mean that international cooperation did not exist. On the contrary, when the debt crisis in Latin America became evident and the international financial system was seriously threatened, the central banks of the major industrial countries demonstrated their flexibility and efficiency. Within days interim financial help for Mexico was organized. The Bank for International Settlements (BIS) in Basel, the bank of the central banks, and the committee of G-10 central bank governors, under the chairmanship of the president of the Swiss national bank, Fritz Leutwiler, all played a crucial role. By the way, Saudi Arabia which was not a G-10 member, participated actively in a number of credit operations.

The IMF, which was still searching for a new role after the breakdown of the BWS, became the center of international cooperation under its managing director Jacques de Larosière. The IMF was one of two Bretton Woods institutions (the other being the World Bank) to provide short-term balance-of-payment credits mainly for industrialized countries. But in a system of floating exchange rates, there was by definition no need for this kind of support. (Britain in 1976 was an exception because of the special situation of sterling as a reserve currency.) Nothing changed the character of the IMF more than the debt crisis and the credit operations that followed, which indeed greatly helped stabilize the financial market and prevented a banking crisis in the United States.

The Fed's tight monetary policy and later the economic and fiscal policy of the Reagan administration led to a renaissance of the dollar, which reached its peak against the deutsche mark in March 1985 when the dollar was worth DM 3.47 compared to DM 1.80 in 1979, before Volcker raised interest rates dramatically. In the meantime, Donald Regan and Beryl Sprinkle were replaced by James Baker and David Mulford, but there were no immediate changes in policy or attitudes as far as the exchange rate policy of the dollar was concerned. The Bundesbank, however, became increasingly embarrassed about the devaluation of the deutsche mark. We believed that a correction was necessary and unavoidable. In March, the Bundesbank surprised the markets by selling some billion U.S. dollars without any warning. The

Americans protested, but the markets were impressed and the dollar declined to more realistic levels.

XI

This was long before the Plaza meeting, held in New York on September 21–22, which in my view was more of a public relations show for home consumption in the United States because the administration wanted to act against increasing protectionist pressure in Congress. The view, which some of the participants expressed later, that the Plaza accord was the beginning of a new phase of international monetary cooperation in my opinion is not justified given the facts.

The Bundesbank was not included in the preparations of the Plaza agreement. They were left entirely to the officials of the finance ministries of the G-5. But the Bundesbank agreed to continue selling reasonable amounts of dollars in a concerted action because we felt that this was in our interest. But there were always tensions and misunderstandings about the character of the agreement with the U.S. Treasury. In hindsight I believe that the Plaza meeting was a nonevent because the dollar was already on the way down, not the least because of the growing U.S. budget deficit, which became an issue of increasing anxiety for the markets.

As far as cooperation in the G-5 was concerned, the Plaza agreement did more harm than good because it made the policymaking process much more visible. From then on, the public expected a communiqué after each meeting of finance ministers and central bank governors—communiqués that over time became more and more meaningless.

Much more important than the Plaza meeting was the Louvre meeting on 22 February 1987. (It was somewhat curious because in the meantime, under heavy political pressure, the G-5 had been enlarged to the G-7 to include Canada and Italy. But the Italians did not participate in the Paris meeting, having protested some protocol measures.) The Americans had prepared a document that included very detailed rules for future intervention in stopping a further decline of the dollar, which in fact had lost almost half of its value in two years. The discussions took a whole day, and by the end we agreed on concerted interventions, but I declared that in my understanding this could not be interpreted as an agreement on target zones or ranges. This statement was completely ignored by all the other participants. In fact, most of the finance ministers gave the impression that the Louvre agreement was the first step toward developing a more rigid system of target zones defended by interventions. This was especially true of our colleagues from the smaller countries, who were expected to participate in market operations but got completely confusing information on what had been agreed to.

XII

The discussions reached their climax at the IMF meeting in September 1987 in Washington, when to my surprise even the British chancellor in his official speech advocated a kind of target zone concept. The French, of course, had always been in favor of fixed exchange rates. What only two or three of the G-7 participants knew was that the Bundesbank had already decided to tighten its monetary policy. The majority of the central bank council became increasingly worried about the outlook for inflation. We didn't want to repeat the mistake we had made at the end of the 1970s regarding the exchange rate situation. Under external pressure, we hesitated too long in making the necessary decisions.

After the IMF meeting, when it became known that the Bundesbank had begun to tighten monetary policy, Secretary of State James Baker made his well-known remark on U.S. television that "The United States would not accept surplus countries raising interest rates"; and the stock markets reacted very nervously. Ironically, Baker, the German finance minister, and I had a peaceful lunch in Frankfurt on October 19, during which I tried to explain the decision of the Bundesbank. When Wall Street opened, the Dow Jones fell 600 points. Later, this day was called "the crash of 1987."

The markets regarded the tensions as a failure of international monetary cooperation. It has, indeed, become obvious that exchange-rate stabilization cannot work if underlying economic fundamentals do not converge. Of course there were a number of reasons for the crash of 1987 much more fundamental than the casual remark of a high government official on a cautious move of German interest rates. As a matter of fact, the Louvre agreement was the last attempt to stabilize the $/DM rate.

So, maybe we have to learn to live with exchange-rate volatility, and maybe it's the lesser evil. Actually, it has become much easier for business to protect themselves against the effects of exchange-rate volatility by using modern financial techniques. Instead of trying to defend exchange rates against strong market forces, it would be useful in my view for the international community to agree on a set of basic principles dealing with monetary policy to achieve a higher degree of convergence. This would also lead to more exchange-rate stability. The G-7 is a useful forum for that purpose, as are the gatherings of central bankers in Basel—discrete, high efficient meetings, as we saw during the debt crisis in 1982 in the field of banking supervision. The IMF can also play a more active role.

I'm strongly opposed to the creation of new institutions, which is always suggested when problems cannot be solved by existing institutions. What we urgently need is an international, liberal spirit to maintain free markets not only for goods and services but also for money and capital, which is so important for the allocation of investments, economic growth, and prosperity.

Of course in a highly integrated single market, which we already have to a remarkable extent in Europe, the issue of exchange-rate stability has a different quality, even more so in a political framework that deserves the ambitious name political union.

2   The Road to European Economic and Monetary Union

I

In the previous chapter I addressed the issue of international cooperation in the areas of monetary policy and currency management, and I said that efforts toward achieving greater exchange-rate stability in Europe began in 1973 at the same time that the BWS collapsed. Indeed, it was earlier in 1971 when the deutsche mark was allowed to float that Karl Schiller, the German economic minister, tried to arrange a kind of European group floating. But the political climate in Europe at the time was close to freezing for reasons that I will not go into here. In 1973 Helmut Schmidt tried again to favor a European bloc because he was very fearful of the political and economic consequences of free floating.

France's finance minister Valery Giscard d'Estaing was immediately ready to participate in such an effort, but the United Kingdom was very reluctant (except for prime minister Edward Heath) because of the role of sterling as a reserve currency. Finally, the "snake" was born, but without British participation (very much like the EMS until 1990). Actually, Helmut Schmidt had offered the British government a credit facility of $5 billion, but fortunately the offer

was not accepted; I am not sure the Bundesbank council
would have agreed, which was necessary because the Bundesbank, not the government, had to provide the credit.
So the snake like the EMS later, became a German-French
arrangement with the participation of several smaller countries. But the French-German axis was fragile. In the turbulent 1970s, France had to leave the snake twice; and in 1978
the snake had practically become a deutsche mark zone,
with a number of smaller countries pegging their currencies to the mark, but it lacked the participation of major
countries such as the United Kingdom and France—very
similar to the situation we have today.

On 11 July 1978, the occasion of a German-French summit meeting in Bremen, Schmidt and Giscard d'Estaing surprised the world (and the Bundesbank) with a proposal to
establish a European monetary system centered around a
currency unit called the ECU (which was both a French and
a Bavarian coin in the old days). More important was the
idea they put forth that after two years members would enter into a second stage where the currency reserves of all
the member states would be pooled, allowing practically
unlimited interventions to defend the exchange rates in the
system. The Bundesbank was alarmed and bluntly refused
to accept such a concept because the central bank council
was concerned that this system could become an inflation-
producing machine. The relationship between the chancellor and the central bank council became so critical that
Schmidt even threatened to change the Bundesbank law
(a completely unrealistic consideration because he would
never have gotten a majority in parliament to do that).

After months of negotiations in both the ministerial council in Brussels and the committee of central bank governors
in Basel, the Bundesbank, Emminger and I finally succeeded in changing the Schmidt-Giscard concept. The sys-

tem became asymmetric, that is the debtor country would have access to generous but limited credit facilities and, most important, credit had to be settled within six months in the currency of the creditor. This rule was slightly expanded in the Basel/Nyborg agreement on 12/13 September 1987, which also includes credits for nonobligatory interventions, but the basic rule still exists today.

II

The Bundesbank's fears that intervention obligations under a system of fixed but adjustable exchange rates would once again, as it did under the Bretton Woods parity regime, undercut its ability to pursue a monetary policy aimed at maintaining price stability may have been exaggerated. After all, the EMS provided for asset settlement after a brief period, and Germany's EMS partners were unlikely to adhere to a kind of "benign neglect" in their exchange-rate policy for other reasons as well, such as concerns about their competitiveness. This made agreement on central rate realignment imperative at the end of the day. Too frequent realignments, however, put the EMS at risk. That changed only in 1983 when France decided to drastically reorient its economic policies in the direction of overall economic balance and monetary stability. France's willingness to accept the inherent logic of a fixed-rate system—quite in line with its own long-standing preference, but without some of the glaring contradictions in its actual application—eliminated the most serious potential threat to the EMS exchange-rate mechanism. This established the foundation for full participation of other EC members that did not enter the exchange-rate mechanism from the start or had opted for the wider 6% fluctuation band. It certainly made it easier for Germany and the Bundesbank to welcome newcomers.

France's change of mind also promised to strengthen the
core group of stability-minded partners, which without
France consisted only of Germany and the Netherlands,
with Belgium and Denmark slowly working their way into
that group.

The gradual acceptance both of the deutsche mark as
the system's key currency and of the Bundesbank's monetary policy as its anchor, though unintentional and reminis-
cent of other key currencies' problems, also helped the EMS
achieve greater cohesion and credibility. With central rates
essentially fixed since 1987 and a growing conviction that
Germany's partners in the core group would resist changes
in their nominal exchange rates against the deutsche mark,
it could be claimed that a quasi-monetary union had come
into existence.

III

Quasi-monetary union was meant to characterize a state of
affairs with near fixed exchange rates between the participants' currencies and de facto acceptance of one monetary
policy by all participants. Of course, exchange rates in the
Exchange Rate Mechanism (of the European Monetary System) ERM were never fixed, since they were fluctuation
bands within which rates could move, and realignments
still remained an option in extreme situations. And key central bank interest rates and other monetary instrument vari-
ables were not identical as they would have been under a
single monetary policy. But interest rate differentials increasingly narrowed. What was really missing in the quasi-
monetary union was a common monetary policy.

Heated debates about the appropriateness of interest rate
or other monetary policy actions taken by the anchor country's central bank at times raised doubts that the imper-

atives of a single monetary policy were already accepted. Indeed, the fact that the single monetary policy was decided by one national central bank rather than a community central bank underlined the reality that full monetary union did not exist.

The essentials of monetary union were already defined in the Werner Report of 1970:

• unlimited and irreversible currency convertibility;

• full liberalization of capital transactions and full integration of banking and financial markets;

• elimination of fluctuation bands and irrevocable fixing of exchange rates.

Free convertibility among the six community currencies, irrevocable fixing of their exchange rates with one another, centralization of monetary and budgetary policies at the community level, a common external monetary policy, complete integration of the members' financial markets, and the adoption of regional policies were all parts of a program laid down in the Werner plan. The plan proved to be far too ambitious at the time. It never got off the ground because the "time was not ripe," and the quasi-monetary union called the EMS failed. In the final analysis, the reason for its failure was the lack of political will to subordinate other objectives to the goal of monetary union, whose main element is of course exchange-rate stability.

IV

The increasing convergence of economic fundamentals paved the road to economic and monetary union, at least in view of some politicians. On 26 February, 1988 German foreign minister Hans Dietrich Genscher (in his capacity as chairman of the Liberal party, not as member of the government—a very strange procedure) published a paper in which he suggested establishing a European currency and a European central bank. The Bundesbank was taken by surprise. But it had to accept it as a basic political proposal, which was finally approved by the cabinet and a broad majority in parliament, including the opposition.

The president of the Bundesbank had no choice but to participate in the negotiations that followed in the Delors committee and try to influence the outcome as much as possible. But he was not excited about contributing to a political project that was intended to move the power of the Bundesbank from the national to the supranational level. The conflict of interest was obvious. So I tried to make the best of it by implementing as much *Bundesbankspirit* into the report as possible. But the Delors report, particularly the appendix, shows how divergent the views about a monetary union (even among central bank governors) had been at that time. That changed later when the governors, without the participation of the commission and noncentral bank experts, agreed on a statute for a future European central bank, which became part of the Maastricht Treaty.

I hold the widely shared view that these arrangements for a future single currency meet the test of a modern monetary constitution (*Geldverfassung* in German). The yardstick commonly applied is the Bundesbank law. It is often pointed out that the statute of the future european system of central banks (ESCB) and the european central bank (ECB) matches the Bundesbank's statute in its commitment to price stability as the overriding objective of monetary policy and to remain above political interference; it also matches it in its single-minded attention to the essentials of monetary policy and its full panoply of instruments required to pursue its objectives. It exceeds it in other respects, for example, the outright denial of central bank financing of government deficits.

The Maastricht Treaty does not define price stability in very precise terms; national central bank governors are to be appointed for a minimum of five years, rather than eight as are executive board members; the rules on exchange rate policy vis-à-vis third countries leave room for ambiguity; and recourse to bank reserve requirements will be subject to the community's secondary legislation. But these are not points on which the Bundesbank law is tougher or more specific. On balance, as far as the monetary union side of the arrangement is concerned, the treaty may not be a central banker's dream, but it also is not his worst nightmare.

One may want to ask: What explains the willingness of the negotiating governments to enshrine firm commitments to price stability and central bank independence in the treaty and back them up with strong elements of self-discipline, especially in the fiscal area? After all, some of these commitments flatly contradict the views defended until now by the majority of member countries at the national level. One explanation could be that in the race to Maastricht the governors of community central banks were given a free hand in preparing the groundwork for the final negotiations at the Intergovernmental Conference on European Monetary Union. (As I stated, it was the committee of central bank governors, without outside assistance, that drafted the statute of the ESBC and the ECB.) But could this really explain the result? Even if the central bank governors could be expected to opt for an independent ESCB and ECB and be totally committed to sound money, would their governments have allowed them to have things their way? Surely something more was at work.

I would like to believe that the real explanation is that most politicians and their electorates have come to accept the basic arguments for price stability and against debasement of the currency, and for central bank independence and against political interference. Some may still believe that a quantum leap in growth and employment might be worth tolerating an additional dose of inflation. But they could not ignore the statistical evidence that shows the gains to be doubtful and ephemeral, while the negative effects of uncontrolled inflation prove to be all too certain and long lasting. There also seems to be greater recognition of the structural and supply-side essentials of permanent higher growth and employment. All this must have raised governments' readiness to let their central bank governors find the necessary common ground at their own level of competence and to build on it when they negotiated the treaty at the intergovernment conference.

Also, Germany's partners may have realized that agreement was only possible on a design that incorporated key elements of the Bundesbank model, with perhaps minor adaptations. In any case, if Germany was going to give up its dominant position and share its monetary anchor role with others, a price had to be paid. The post-Maastricht debate in Germany suggests that large sections of the population may not be willing to give up the deutsche mark at any price, not even if a Bundesbank-type European central bank is accepted by its partners.

V

It is hard to tell how durable the anti-inflationary consensus in Europe will be. There are signs that it may have reached its high point and that other economic policy goals are becoming more relevant, in particular, reducing unemployment and encouraging growth. But pushing ahead with EMU at precisely the time when the stability consensus seemed most secure may well imply that a unique opportunity was not seized, an opportunity to give Europe a monetary constitution based on principles that, at other times, governments and parliaments might be less willing to accept. Once in place, the monetary constitution flanked by other irreversible institutional steps would in turn provide assurances against the emergence of cracks in the stability consensus, at least up to a point.

It seemed that by signing the Maastricht Treaty all twelve governments demonstrated their countries' readiness to accept the required wholesale transfer of monetary sovereignty from the national to the community level. But such declarations were made subject to ratification of the new treaty in all member countries in accordance with national constitutional provisions, as required under Article 236 of the Treaty of Rome and under the new Article 102a introduced by the Unified European Act in 1987. This seemed no more than a formality. The negative vote in the Danish referendum on 2 June 1992 was a total surprise even to those close at hand and caused widespread consternation. It found the European Commission totally unprepared to deal with this unexpected turn and provoked a number of disturbing reactions. Among them was the view that Denmark had catapulted itself outside the community because it had rejected a new treaty that replaced the old one, rather than treaty amendments. The British gave proof of their sang-froid. They promptly halted the ratification process in their Parliament, arguing that it could only be resumed after certain questions raised by the Danish referendum had been settled. Finally, both Denmark and the United Kingdom have reserved their right to ratify the treaty and have made it very clear that they are not ready to give up their national sovereignty in certain areas, particularly in monetary policy.

Germany very characteristically has made the treaty subject to a vote of its constitutional court. Its position is a strong "yes, but. . . ." Germany has actually raised the prerequisites for participation in the EMU ("convergence criteria") so high that for the time being no country in Europe is able to meet them.

VI

Thus one could argue that the creation of an European Monetary Institute (EMI) has academic rather than practical relevance. It will only continue the work of the committee of central bank governors, and it can try to develop tools for a common monetary policy if and when the time comes (for instance, agreed definitions of monetary targets). But it has no decisionmaking power, and it has already been called an "empty shell."

I do not believe this is fair. Further work is necessary because the provisions of the ESCB statute enshrined in the Maastricht Treaty leave room for different approaches. When considering the issue in all its complexity, the council of EMI may wish to take note of what Harry Johnson had to say in 1971. "The individual central banks will have to surrender whatever trappings and substance of autonomy they still possess, and become mere delegates to a central policy making conference. This will be hard for the proud tradition of national central banking." [1]

---

1. *Euromoney*, Vol. 2, No. 11, April 1971, pp. 39–43, reprinted in Harry G. Johnson, *Further Essays in Monetary Economics* (London: 1972), pp. 312–324.

There are those who see the future ESCB as a very loose congregation of national central banks that will allow the central banks much leeway in implementing the very general monetary policy directives agreed to at the level of the ESCB's governing council meetings held from time to time, on annual targets for an appropriate monetary aggregate, or on key central bank interest rates. To defend this position, reference is sometimes made to subsidiarity as a guiding treaty principle. This points to a serious misconception of the role and modus operandi of monetary policy. It is interesting to note that insistence on subsidiarity as a governing principle even in the monetary area seems most vocal in countries with highly centralized central banking structures. This suggests there may be hidden motives, among them perhaps the belief that the interests of national financial systems or centers will be best served if the national central bank retains ample room to maneuver within a loose European central bank structure.

As far as monetary policy autonomy is concerned, the experience of the period since the Werner plan strongly supports what Johnson claimed in 1971, namely that the "integration of world financial markets already imposes severe constraints on the freedom of individual countries to pursue really independent monetary policies."

VII

Indeed, the 1970s and 1980s might well be called the decades of financial market integration. For a growing number of community countries, participation in the exchange-rate mechanism of the EMS amounted to an open admission that, even after the breakdown at the ERM, acceptance of such constraints by way of tying their currency to the deutsche mark offered greater chances of success in achieving price stability than insistence on preserving what little was left of their monetary autonomy in a world of closely integrated financial markets.

For most countries participating in the exchange-rate mechanism of the EMS, borrowing the Bundesbank's credibility as a successful guardian of price stability has truly paid off. As a result, the community as a whole has gone through an impressive process of greater convergence of inflation rates at substantially reduced levels. Without this achievement, the decision to rapidly move forward on the road to EMU could not have been taken. Indeed, full success in achieving price stability in the community (or among the participants of the ERM) was likely to increase pressure to transform the EMS through institutional changes that would meet the other partner's desire to share responsibility for the community's monetary policy, rather than leave decisions solely to the central bank of one of its partners.

Last but not least, the speed with which poorer countries were able to catch up with their richer partners in the quest for greater cohesion has also slowed down recently. Backsliding, rather than progress in key integration areas, does not augur well for EMU; nor does the temptation to blame the Bundesbank's monetary policy for problems caused by German unification, a situation where huge public sector deficits, high wage costs, and excessive money growth lead to higher interest rates in Europe than they might have been otherwise.

VIII

If the commitments made in the Maastricht Treaty are to be taken seriously, the ESCB's monetary policy would not differ very much in nature from that of the Bundesbank. The only difference would be that the ESCB would pursue the goal of price stability for the whole economic area. Relative prices would then adjust more readily than under the rules of behavior of the EMS, with Germany resisting inflation and other partners resisting exchange-rate adjustment vis-à-vis the deutsche mark. To pursue the argument to its logical conclusion, it has sometimes been suggested that "The European economy would be healthier if the DMark had been allowed to appreciate in real terms after reunification."[2]

In fact, that happened in the markets by a decision of governments; and as a result interest rates in some countries were allowed to decline substantially. But some of Germany's partners still fear devaluation like the devil fears holy water, where in the past devaluation was all too often seen as the easy way out of difficulties.

The proponents of EMU and of the ECU have a kind of dream that the community's future single currency will become one of the pillars of a future international monetary system, based on the dollar, yen, and ECU. But it would be a dangerous illusion to believe that a future single currency—called ECU or something more attractive—will automatically inherit the deutsche mark's international role.

The ESCB will have to build the necessary credibility not only inside the community, but also outside it. It will have to calm fears that it will pursue an easier monetary policy with lower interest rates where the Bundesbank would have refused to. Otherwise, international investors will quickly decide to move their funds into other currencies.

The best technical solutions will not eliminate the need to ensure that EMU gets off the ground with participating

---

2. Peter Kenen, "Speaking up for EMU," *Financial Times,* 28 July 1992.

countries' economies in reasonably good shape and with as few risks stacked up against success as possible. The global environment is not likely to help much, unless economic growth picks up soon without increasing inflation. And progress toward closer convergence and cohesion has all but stopped, if it has not yet been reversed. As I stated at the outset, circumstances may have seemed favorable to restarting the integration process in the 1980s; but they may not be as favorable for its implementation.

This suggests that as a minimum condition for success, or as an insurance against disaster, participation in EMU from the start of stage three should be strictly limited to members that offer adequate assurance that their inflation rate, fiscal deficit, and public debt, as well as other relevant factors, will not be causes of discord and tension from the beginning. I have long favored a multiple speed approach that would allow a core group to move ahead fully confident of success, while allowing others to join as they meet the necessary entry criteria. This has been the formula actually applied in the EMS, although without predetermined criteria for participation.

IX

According to German expert legal opinion expressed in a vote by the German constitutional court, fundamental democratic principles have been neglected so far in the community: EC legislation does not originate in a democratically elected parliament, but from the commission and the council of ministers. The executive assumes the role of the legislative; it makes decisions behind closed doors and discourages public control by insisting on complicated language and procedures. The result is obfuscation. The treaty itself has been criticized for its opaque language.

The issue of political union is not one of fiscal policy only, or even primarily. There are arguments on both sides of the question: Does a single monetary policy call for closely co-ordinated or even centralized decisionmaking in other areas as well, particularly in fiscal policy? Obviously yes, but too much fiscal power in the hands of the Brussels authorities, especially if insufficiently controlled by a European parliament, could cause greater problems for the common monetary policy than decentralized budget decisions made at the national level.

And what will be the role of a European parliament with decisionmaking power on taxation and expenditure? From the point of view of contributor countries, this scenario is not without its problems if they have no veto rights.

X

So the Maastricht Treaty has been ratified by all member states, but many questions still have to be answered. In my view, the treaty to some extent deals more with the Europe of the past than the Europe of the future. It has become very obvious that the concept of a centralized ("federalistic") Europe with decisionmaking powers increasingly being transferred into the hands of a European bureaucracy behaving like a European government and controlled by a 1,000-member parliament is neither realistic nor desirable. What we should aim for is a Europe without barriers for goods and services, money and capital, and—difficult enough—people. We should also recognize that with the fall of communism Europe no longer ends at the river Elbe or even at the Oder. Poland, the Czech republic, Hungary, and others must be included in the European Community, one way or another. And this will change the character of the EC completely.

As far as monetary arrangements are concerned, fixed exchange rates and, as a consequence, a single currency are certainly no longer the main preoccupation of some governments. The real issues are and will continue to be unemployment, which has reached alarming numbers in all European countries, including Germany and free trade worldwide (GATT) as well as within Europe. The more unemployment rises, the stronger the tendency toward protectionism. International cooperation in the 1970s and 1980s did not produce a new international monetary order like the Bretton Woods system, and even the EMS system, close to a de facto monetary union, finally collapsed. If fixed or at least stable exchange rates had been an aim in itself, the last twenty years of international and European monetary policy could be called a history of failure.

It was possible, however, to maintain the freedom of markets and, as far as Europe is concerned, many barriers have been abolished. A single market is not a distant goal but a reality for the core of Europe. This is much more than a free trade area. It is the economic basis for Europe an success in a world of increasing international competition. If markets continue to integrate, this could finally lead to a single currency and a common monetary policy. A single currency, however, must first be a stable currency because sound money is the most important basis for economic growth and prosperity.

As the communiqué of the London summit in 1977 stated—and I have to admit that I was one of the authors of that sentence, which could soon become relevant again—"Inflation is not a remedy for unemployment, but one of its main causes."

Appendix: The Further Development of the European Monetary System

I Introduction

With the planned creation of an integrated financial market with free movement of capital, a basic component of a future monetary union would also exist. An additional basic element, namely firmly fixed exchange rates, is admittedly not a prospect within the foreseeable future because setbacks in coordinating economic policy can no more be excluded than can disturbances in the financial markets and the real economy, which can make exchange rate adjustments necessary. Corrections in exchange rates will remain a necessary safety valve for the foreseeable future also within the EMS in order to reduce any tensions that may arise without incurring excessive damage to individual economies or the community as a whole. Even the unification of the markets to form a single European market does not necessarily presuppose the existence of a monetary union or a common currency. Nevertheless, the time may have come to develop some concrete ideas about the process of integration that can lead to a monetary union.

A number of recent proposals seek to anticipate the emergence of new conflicts between the common objective of exchange-rate stability and national notions of price stability through a quantum leap, by coupling the commitment to achieve a single European market and an integrated financial space with freedom of capital movements by 1992 with the creation of a European central bank. From the German point of view it is essential to ensure, in the discussions about the future design of a European monetary order, that monetary and credit policy is not geared to stability to a lesser extent in an economically united Europe than it is today in Germany. Apart from this, it should be made clear that monetary integration cannot move ahead of general economic integration, since the whole process of integration would be burdened with considerable economic and social tensions. Moreover, examples from history demonstrate that new nations did not confer a uniform monetary order on themselves until after the process of unification was concluded. Any durable attempt to fix exchange rates within the community and finally to replace national currencies by a European currency would be doomed to failure as long as a minimum of policy shaping and decisionmaking in the field of economic and fiscal policy does not take place at the community level. Without this prerequisite being met, a common European monetary policy cannot ensure monetary stability on its own. Above all, it cannot paper over the problems in the community arising from differing economic and fiscal policies.

The following considerations begin with the basic elements of an economic and monetary union (EMU). The thread cannot simply be picked up with the ideas contained in the Werner Report as long ago as 1970, namely to move toward this goal via a multi-stage plan. With the "snake" and the EMS, experience has been gained, and with the progress in economic and monetary policy cooperation, facts have been created which suggest the need for a new start. In this context, it must be ensured from the outset that agreement exists between the governments and the community institutions for which they are responsible with respect to the basic issues of economic policy. Above all, agreement must exist that stability of the value of money is the indispensable prerequisite for the achievement of other goals. Particular importance therefore will be attached to the principles on which a European monetary order should be based.

Drawing partially on preliminary work conducted within the community on the second stage of the EMS, three models of monetary integration are presented and examined with respect to their compatibility with the demands of a future monetary union. The models that have been selected take ideas into account that play a role in political discussions or could play a role in them at any time. Since it can be assumed that the goal of monetary union cannot be reached in a quantum jump but only as the result of a process of integration encompassing economic and monetary policy, individual conceivable stages of integration with their political implications are taken into consideration. The problems arising from the differing speed of integration on the part of individual countries as well as from the institutional and legal aspects of integration are also discussed.

II   The Final Objective of Monetary Integration

A   Economic and Monetary Integration

1   *The Characteristics of a Monetary Union*
The final objective of monetary union was defined as early as 1970 in the Werner Report in a formulation that still applies today: "A monetary union implies inside its boundaries the total and irreversible convertibility of currencies,

the elimination of margins of fluctuation in exchange rates, the irrevocable fixing of parity rates and the complete liberation of movements of capital." The decisive criteria for a monetary union are thus the irrevocable fixing of exchange rates and movements of capital within the single monetary area that are free from restrictions. The monetary union is the monetary superstructure of the economic union in which the four freedoms have been realized, namely the free movement of goods, services, labor, and capital. Within the common single market, economic activity is to be based on a free market system of competition. Besides agreement on regulative policy, an economic union demands a far-reaching harmonization of government regulations in order to bring about equal competitive conditions and uniform markets. Although structural and regional differences between the member countries (especially differences in income and productivity) are compatible with an economic union, the structural and regional policy of the community must take them into account.

In principle, national currencies can be retained in the monetary union. However, the introduction of a uniform monetary symbol would give the union a monetary identity, eliminate the residual risk of parity changes among the national currencies, and hence assure the continuing existence of a single monetary area. The replacement of national currencies by a common currency would indeed be the crowning act of the process of monetary integration.

Above and beyond the integration effects of a single European market, a monetary union provides a number of additional economic advantages. First, the irrevocable fixing of parities means that the exchange rate risk associated with the intra-community exchange of goods, services, and capital is eliminated. This will foster, in particular, the integration of the financial markets and the strengthening of competition. Second, there will be a saving in transaction costs since market participants will be increasingly willing to accept partner currencies or the common currency without taking recourse to hedging operations and to hold them as a means of payment or investment in the place of national currencies. Third, the creation of a monetary area with a greater weight internationally entails advantages in transactions with third countries since the international acceptance of the community currencies will grow, the community will become less susceptible to external shocks, and it will be able to represent its monetary policy interests more effectively at the international level. The introduction of a common currency would allow full advantage to be drawn from these benefits.

2   Implications for Economic Policy

Within the monetary union, economic policy must be directed toward eliminating causes of tension that could jeopardize its cohesion and toward preventing new tensions from arising. The irrevocable fixing of parity rates is possible only on the basis of exchanges rates at which differences in rates of price increase, balance-of-payments positions, and in the field of public finances have been eliminated to a large extent. With fixed exchange rates, insufficient convergence in these three fields would give rise to adjustment constraints in the real economy that would endanger the cohesion of the monetary union or would ultimately bring about adjustments in parities forcefully. The harmonization of rates of inflation at the lowest possible level is necessary since any shifts that may arise in terms of price competitiveness can no longer be offset by realignments. Countries with an above-average rate of inflation would suffer competitive losses; conversely, tendencies toward excess demand would be triggered in countries with cost advantages.

When parity relationships are irrevocably fixed, the external positions of the partner countries must be compatible with each other since competitive weaknesses of one partner would burden the aggregate balance-of-payments position of the monetary union vis-à-vis the rest of the world. Even if the current account position of the monetary union were in balance as a whole, it would not be possible for a single country within the community to rely indefinitely on capital inflows and the corresponding growth of indebtedness. Finally, there would have to be a large degree of convergence in the field of public finance. Considerable, or even unlimited, recourse by a member state (or the central authority) to central bank credit would make monetary control throughout the monetary area difficult, if not impossible, and—no matter how they are financed—excessive national budget deficits would burden the overall current account position of the monetary union.

Securing convergence within the monetary union—initially with the retention of national currencies—will imply losses in independence in terms of national economic policy, that is, a shift of responsibilities from the national to the community level. This applies to fiscal, economic, social, and wages policy as well as—to a particularly marked extent—to monetary policy: ideally, within the monetary union national currencies are perfect substitutes, that is, market participants are indifferent as regards the various existing currencies. The irrevocable fixing of parity rates under conditions of complete freedom of capital movements implies that national interest rate levels must converge (apart from minor differences arising from market imperfections). Thus it will no longer be possible to conduct an independent national monetary policy that is geared to a national standard.

The basic stance of monetary policy must be laid down by a coordinating body at the community level. National central banks will then only be executive organs for the community's monetary policy. To the extent that they are able to achieve the operational objectives laid down by the community, the harmonization of their instruments initially will not be necessary. In any case, this will be possible only within limits in the preliminary stages since there are wider differences in existing structures of national money, credit, and capital markets that will not disappear immediately even after the complete liberalization of capital movements. However, owing to differing national transmission mechanisms of monetary policy as well as structural differences in the demand for money, it will be possible to achieve a uniform policy for monetary growth that is geared to a monetary target for the community only gradually. Thus, as far as its practical application is concerned, national differences will persist. The creation of a uniform European monetary market that the central authority responsible for monetary policy can manage with its own instruments will, however, be necessary at the latest when a common currency is introduced.

Monetary policy coordination needs to be complemented by the transfer of responsibility for monetary relationships with the rest of the world to the community level since the exchange rates of the partner currencies must develop uniformly. Exchange-rate policy vis-à-vis third countries therefore must be laid down at the community level, interventions on the foreign exchange market be decided jointly (with intervention operations perhaps being centralized at a national central bank or common fund for reasons of expediency), and monetary reserves be pooled. In the field of international monetary policy the community would act as a single entity. Instead of individual countries, it would then also need to be a member of the IMF. Whereas the national states would necessarily lose their monetary policy independence in a monetary union, they can quite easily retain certain responsibilities in the field of fiscal and economic policy, as is the case in every federation of the states. However, in order to exclude any doubts about the cohesion of the monetary union from the outset and at the same time avoid an overburdening of monetary policy, it must be ensured that there is sufficient conformity of action in fiscal and economic policy within the community. This is because any lack of convergence that could give rise to expectations of parity changes would need to be bridged through interventions and interest rate measures on the national money markets in order to ensure the continuing existence of the monetary or exchange rate union. Over time it will thus be necessary to allow for the necessary transfer of economic and fiscal policy responsibilities from national authorities to community organs.

In order to optimize economic policy as a whole, the overall economic objectives for the monetary area should be laid down at the community level. Broad agreement would also need to be reached on the policy mix, that is, the combination of fiscal and monetary policy appropriate for achieving the overall economic objectives. This would also provide a basic guideline for each country's fiscal policy. Moreover, together with the creation of a single European market, a far-reaching—but not necessarily complete—harmonization of indirect taxes would be necessary in order to avoid competitive distortions. Given the existing low degree of mobility of income learners, direct taxes do not need to be harmonized to the same extent; with unchanged shares of expenditure in GNP by the public sector, the harmonization of indirect taxes will also create a need to adjust direct taxes as well as the overall burden of levies.

In light of existing structural imbalances within the community, when parity rates are irrevocably fixed it will be necessary to put in place a system of fiscal compensation through a community organ in favor of the structurally weak member countries. Transfer payments would compensate the weaker members for the burdens of adjustment associated with the definitive renouncement of devaluations as a means of maintaining their competitiveness. Thus, within the monetary union, balance-of-payments policy is replaced by regional policy, with the latter helping to finance interregional differences in current account imbalances through transfer payments. The differences in the level of economic development of individual member countries of the community suggest that extremely large amounts of funds would be needed to finance the necessary fiscal compensation. Only through a very effective regional policy could these differences perhaps be reduced to an extent that would be compatible with the existence of a monetary union.

Incomes policy must also take into account the fixing of parity rates within the monetary union. Divergences in regional developments (such as differing rates of increase in productivity or shifts in demand) require a correspondingly differentiated development of wages in so far as they are not offset by fiscal adjustment within the community. Although regional imbalances can be offset through the mobility of the factors of production, this kind of adjustment would be associated with a shifting of capital and labor out of the less competitive regions which would be undesirable in terms of regional policy (and which, owing to the far lesser degree of mobility of labor, would not occur without friction). Thus, given diverging developments in competitiveness, renouncing exchange-rate adjustments will require a differentiated wages policy, which would also need to cover ancillary wage costs. In branches of industry that manufacture their products under widely similar conditions, a harmonization of nominal wage developments is to be expected within the monetary union in the absence of which diverging rates of inflation could arise. For this reason, even before the inception of the monetary union, the basic willingness of both sides of industry to pursue a wages and incomes policy geared to the operating conditions of such a union must exist, especially bearing in mind that an increasing orientation of wage demands toward the highest level in the community is to be expected within the monetary union. However, given the independent right to conclude collective wage agreements that is appropriate in an economic union based on the rules of free competition, the scope for economic policy to directly affect the development of wages and salaries is very restricted. Everything, therefore, will ultimately depend on a credible and rigorously pursued monetary policy that limits the scope for passing on cost increases and hence prevents excessive increases in nominal wages from occurring.

The economic policy implications of a monetary union can be summed up as follows: A monetary union presupposes considerable shifts in the responsibility for economic policy to a central authority and hence a far-reaching reshaping of the community in political and institutional terms in the direction of a broader union. Although complete political union is not absolutely necessary for the establishment of a monetary union, the loss of national sovereignty in economic and monetary policy associated with it is so serious that it would probably be bearable only in the context of extremely close and irrevocable political integration. In any event, within a monetary union, monetary policy can only be conducted at the community level. A substantial transfer of authority will also be necessary in the field of fiscal policy.

B   Principles of a European Monetary Order

Eschewing technical institutional and monetary details, the following section outlines the decisive principles that absolutely must be taken into account when setting up a European central bank system. (For the sake of simplification, the point of departure is the final stage of monetary integration, namely the transition to a common European currency. However, the following criteria must also be fulfilled already at the stage when the monetary union is created, that is, the irrevocable fixing of the parity rates of national currencies.) The following principles appear to be indispensable:

1. The mandate of the central bank must be to maintain stability of the value of money as the prime objective of European monetary policy. While fulfilling this task, the central bank has to support general economic policy as laid down at the community level. Domestic stability of the value of money must take precedence over exchange-rate stability. This does not exclude the possibility that depreciation vis-à-vis third currencies and the associated import of inflation be counteracted by appropriate monetary policy measures. In the event of the establishment of an

international monetary system with limited exchange-rate flexibility vis-à-vis third currencies, the central bank would need to be given at the least the right to participate in discussions on parity changes.

2. The overriding commitment to maintaining the stability of the value of money must be safeguarded through the central bank's independence of instructions from national governments and community authorities. This simultaneously requires the personal independence of the members of the respective organs, assured by their being appointed to office for a period of at least eight to ten years without the possibility of their being removed from office for political reasons.

3. All the member countries would need to be represented in the monetary policy decisionmaking body, with voting power being weighted in the light of the economic importance of the member countries.

4. A federal structure of the central bank system—according to the pattern of the Federal Reserve System, for instance—would correspond best to the existing state of national sovereignty and additionally would strengthen the independence of the central bank. (Before the final stage involving the introduction of a uniform currency, only a federally structured central bank system is conceivable in any case.)

5. The financing of public sector deficits by the central bank (apart from occasional cash advances) makes effective monetary control impossible over the long term. For a European central bank to be able to fulfill its mandate to ensure monetary stability, strict limitations must be imposed on its granting credit to public authorities of all kinds (including community authorities). This also applies to indi-

rect government financing through the granting of credit to any central bank of the member countries that continue to exist.

6. The European central bank must be equipped with the monetary policy instruments to enable it to manage the money supply effectively without recourse to quantitative controls (or other forms of direct intervention in the workings of the financial markets). Interest rate and liquidity policy instruments must be available both for the general management and for the fine tuning of the European money market.

7. The European central bank should be given the right to take part in the establishment of general regulations in the field of banking supervision. Moreover, owing to its expertise, deriving in particular from its business relations with credit institutions, the central bank should be closely involved in day-to-day banking supervisory activities.

III Models of Monetary Integration

A   European Monetary Fund

The further development of the European Monetary Cooperation Fund (EMCF) to form a European Monetary Fund (EMF) as a kind of regional IMF probably comes closest to the concept the architects of the EMS had in mind, seeing that in accordance with the resolution of the European Council of 5 December 1978 the final system was to be characterized by "the creation of the European Monetary Fund as well as the full utilization of the ECU as a reserve asset and a means of settlement." In addition, the existing credit mechanisms would be consolidated into a single fund.

Moreover, in conjunction with the conclusions relating to monetary policy reached at the meeting of the European Council in Bremen on 6 and 7 July 1978, besides U.S. dollars and gold, "member currencies in an amount of a comparable order of magnitude" were to be brought into the fund. In the discussions in the years 1981–82 about the entry of the EMS into the final stage, it was assumed that this could also involve a final transfer of reserves.

A regional reserve fund with functions similar to those of the IMF would put this institution in a position to become involved in the process of balance-of-payments adjustment and financing on the part of its members. In this way, it could help to avoid recourse being taken to measures that disturb or delay the process of integration in the event of balance-of-payments difficulties. In the opinion of the proponents of such a fund solution, the use of such balance-of-payments assistance as well as the resources made available by the fund for the specific purpose of financing interventions could at the same time also help to stabilize exchange-rate relationships within the EMS. If, in the course of monetary integration, it should come about that national external payments balances cease to exist and there is only a community external payments balance instead, then the fund would have to support the process of adjustment and financing of the balance of payments with its resources.

In the case of a fund along the lines of a regional IMF whose policy would be primarily directed toward safeguarding the external balance of the community member countries as well as exchange-rate stability, the question arises as to the extent to which such a policy would also foster convergence within the community on the basis of price stability. This possibility only exists in the case of conditional balance-of-payments credits being granted, that is, when the consequences of insufficient convergence have already become evident. At stages prior to this, especially when providing resources for intervention purposes without any conditions attached, it could not impose any convergence constraints in the direction of noninflationary growth in the community. The danger that within the EMS the orientation toward domestic stability would be pushed into the background in favor of external stability is obvious. Since the general thrust and coordination of economic, fiscal, and monetary policy would play a role in this model of a fund only at the margin (when conditional credits are granted) the stability-oriented monetary policy of the hard currency countries could be undermined. Moreover, mixing central bank functions together with areas of government responsibility within a single fund bars the way to a European central bank with a decisionmaking body that is independent of governments, and thus should be rejected.

B   A European Parallel Currency

1. As an alternative to the gradual evolution toward a European monetary union—on the basis of greater economic policy convergence, closer coordination of monetary policy and diminishing recourse to exchange-rate realignments—the concept of a parallel currency has been under discussion since the mid-1970s. According to this concept, the driving force behind the process of integration should be the market, not initiatives taken by national governments or community authorities.

Alongside national currencies, an additional community currency would be put into circulation that can fulfill all the functions of money (a means of payment, a unit of account, and a store of value) as far as possible. The parallel currency would be designed in such a way that—without being given preferential treatment—it would be able not only to maintain its position alongside the national currencies but also to gradually crowd out the individual national currencies in line with the generally accepted pace of integration. With the growing importance of the parallel currency, the national central banks would increasingly lose their scope for autonomous monetary policy action in favor of a community central bank institution, since a growing proportion of the money in circulation in each country would no longer be under national control. Thus, there would be a de facto loss of independence in the sphere of national monetary policy without the need for any explicit shift in responsibilities to the community level. This process would end with the abolition of the national currencies through a special sovereign act and the introduction of a single European currency.

Compared with the well-known difficulties of progressively restricting national responsibility for economic policy through political acts, the idea of a parallel currency may appear to be quite elegant at first sight. It would meet with the desire to undertake politically effective and symbolic steps (such as introducing a European currency, including the issuing of banknotes and coins, and setting up a European central bank) without a major need to relinquish sovereignty rights at the outset. However, on closer inspection it becomes evident that this approach also requires an immediate and far-reaching need for changes in institutional terms if the currency competition that is set in motion is to proceed in a way that is acceptable for all the member countries. In this context, a large number of open and very complex questions arise. Agreement can be expressed with a recent study on the European monetary system, which states that "the full logical implications of this approach were never drawn up at the official level."[1]

2. Currency competition between the national currencies and a parallel currency can arise only if the latter is placed on an equal footing with all national currencies with respect to their relevant functions. Besides the envisaged complete liberalization of capital movements, that is, the free use of each national currency and a parallel currency in external transactions, there would have to be equality of status for each national currency within the domestic economy as well. To ensure a sufficient degree of acceptance of the parallel currency as a means of payments, its utilization would have to be permissible for domestic transactions as well; however, its full recognition as legal tender would not appear to be necessary. A harmonization of exchange-rate regulations would be required beforehand lest an undesirable uneven distribution of the parallel currency come about from the start.

3. The economic effects of the introduction of a parallel currency depend on the concrete aspects of its design. On the basis of the existing European monetary unit, the ECU, a large number of parallel currency concepts in part with widely differing implications can be conceived of depending in each case on the criteria that are decisive—an independent status for the ECU as opposed to a basket definition, exchange-rate regulations, and the role to be played by central banks. As points of reference, two interim solutions of practical relevance constituting, on the one hand, the issuing of ECUs at the national level and, on the other

1. Daniel Gros and Niels Thygesen, *The EMS: Achievements, Current Issues and Directions for the Future* (Brussels: 1988).

hand, their being issued at the community level are presented below: in the first case, the ECU is defined, as it exists now, as a basket of currencies with a fixed but adjustable exchange rate (See type 1); in the second case, the ECU is an independently defined unit that would be put into circulation as an additional currency with a fixed but adjustable exchange rate (type 2).

By contrast, the present state (a basket ECU with a fixed but adjustable exchange rate[2] without the systematic involvement of central banks in the private creation of ECUs) as well as the final state of a de facto monetary union (basket ECU or independently defined ECU with an absolutely fixed exchange rate) are not analyzed in detail.[3] As far as the present state is concerned, on the basis of experience the purely private circulation of ECUs (which is only possible on the basis of a basket ECU) is of limited significance and such a restricted role of the ECU will not contribute toward monetary integration. Section II dealt extensively with the final state. In the case of immutably fixed exchange rates vis-à-vis the national currencies, the ECU would not be a parallel currency but a dual currency; monetary union then would not be an objective still to be attained by means of the parallel currency but would already exist. The difference between an independently defined ECU and a basket ECU would be meaningless in the final state so that this case does not need to be discussed any further.

4. As already mentioned above, the parallel currency approach seeks to approach the final state of monetary union

---

2. Ignoring the special role of the lira, sterling, and the drachma.
3. The independently defined ECU with a flexible exchange rate (type 3) propagated in scientific circles is also not examined because, although it is a model with theoretical advantages, it cannot be considered a realistic alternative.

over the longer term through currencies competing with each other and with the ECU.[4] For the parallel currency to have a chance in the competition among currencies, it must be attractive from the point of view of individual economic agents as an investment currency (i.e., the net yield from the development of interest rates and exchange rates must be able to compete with the net yield obtainable on assets invested in a national currency) and should not be inferior to the national currency as a transaction currency (i.e., the transaction costs and the exchange rate risk involved in cash management must be as low as possible). To the extent that a crowding out of the national currency occurs, this process must operate in the right direction, that is, good money must not be replaced by bad money (Gresham's Law) if price stability is to be maintained. How competition between the individual currencies actually develops and what monetary policy implications can be associated with it depends crucially on the way the parallel currency is designed in each case.

a. The Basket ECU as a Parallel Currency (Type 1)   As things stand today, the use of the basket ECU as a parallel currency while retaining fixed but adjustable exchange rates vis-à-vis the individual national currencies appears to be the most obvious approach. The decisive step toward the introduction of such a parallel currency would consist of

4. It appears doubtful whether all member countries would be prepared to engage in unrestricted competition among currencies with all its consequences, including large-scale crowding out of the national currency. It can probably be realistically assumed that national monetary authorities do not want to risk their currencies being crowded out of circulation in the domestic economy and will therefore keep the extent to which the parallel currency spreads under control by restricting its use in one way or the other.

making it possible for ECUs to be created by the national central banks (in accordance with uniform directives) or by a community monetary authority. The basket ECU would then be created not only—as is currently the case—by the private bundling of the individual components but also through the granting of credit or intervention operations by the central banks or a community monetary authority.

Under the conditions described above, (apart from third currencies) twelve national EC currencies and the basket ECU as an investment and external transaction currency, together with two domestic transactions and accounting units, would be available to the citizens of the EC. With fixed but adjustable exchange rates, the use of the basket ECU would be suitable as a diversification instrument, being the weighted average of the national currencies it cannot be superior to all other individual currencies or mixtures of currencies. With freedom of capital movements and persistent divergences within the EMS, it is quite possible that for a number of reasons the deutsche mark will be generally preferred as an investment currency and will crowd out both the ECU and other national currencies. Although with an increasing degree of convergence among the EC currencies, the deutsche mark will lose some of its relatively greater attractiveness for nonresidents; the diversification motive for the ECU-denominated investments will lose importance at the same time. Investments denominated in other community currencies would tend to be less profitable in the eyes of investors in each country so that in both cases little argues in favor of investment denominated in ECU.

The ability of the ECU as a transaction currency to crowd out national currencies within the domestic economy cannot be judged in much more positive terms either.

Especially in the case of foreseeable divergences, the exchange-rate risk involved would impair the use of the ECU for day-to-day transactions, for example through the constant need to determine exchange rates, irritating conversion rates, and greater difficulty in agreeing on prices between domestic contractual partners who would have to take possible exchange-rate risks into account if the contract is denominated in ECU. Even in the event of greater convergence, habits, the acquired memory of prices in national currency, and similar factors tend to argue against the spread of the ECU. Thus, on balance, the best that can be expected is that the ECU would be increasingly used in intra-community trade as a compromise currency, whereby, however, the crucial factor would probably not least be the negotiating position of the business partners concerned.

As a weighted average of national currencies, a basket ECU can therefore not exert any durable and especially any symmetrical pressure in the direction of crowding out national currencies, and hence cannot be seen as an additional instrument for bringing about integration either. Precisely with respect to the fact that the attractiveness of a basket ECU is not assured as far as individual economic agents are concerned, it can be assumed that the EC central banks would be obliged to stabilize the exchange rate of such an ECU through unlimited purchases in order to foster the use of the ECU.[5] Should ECUs circulate on a relatively large scale, such an intervention obligation would have important consequences for monetary policy; in the final

---

5. If, as is assumed, all the basket currencies are part of a system of fixed, but adjustable exchange rates, then intervention points for the basket ECU vis-à-vis each individual national currency can be derived from their bilateral intervention points.

analysis, it would be tantamount to undertaking unlimited purchases of partner currencies without settlement and bringing about the integration of the circulation of official and private ECUs. If the market wanted to exchange ECUs for national currency then this would depress the exchange rate of the ECU against the currency in question. Through purchases to support the ECU the desired national currency will then be made available. As a result, ECU holdings would accumulate with the central banks whose currencies are in stronger demand than the currencies of its partners (or ECU), whereas the central banks responsible for issuing the currencies that are less in demand would have to issue ECUs by purchasing their own currency. On the assumption that divergences exist within the EMS, a de facto asymmetrical crowding out of the national currencies concerned within Europe would come about. The national stability policy of the hard currency countries would be undermined. National price objectives would necessarily have to be sacrificed to the average rate of inflation in Europe. For these reasons, such a concept alone requires management of the money supply at the European level in order to ensure an equal rate of money creation (ECU plus national currency). Only in this way would it be possible to avoid a dual coverage of GDP in Europe through the circulation of ECUs and national currencies.

Moreover, redesigning the existing ECU to form a parallel currency would make it difficult to statistically record the national money supply if ECU bank notes were to be issued.[6] Although it would be known how many ECU

---

6. In case an ECU parallel currency were introduced, ECU banknotes would probably be issued even if the ECU were not to be declared legal tender.

bank notes had been issued all in all, it would not be known how many of them are actually held in Germany or any other country. In addition, there would be exchange-rate-induced fluctuation in the national money supply expressed in terms of national currency. Finally, account would also need to be taken of the general possibility that already exists today of shifting funds into offshore centers; this might possibly play an even greater role for holdings of ECUs than is the case with respect to national currencies. These reservations apply in equal measure to the independently defined ECU that is discussed below.

b. An Independently Defined ECU as a Parallel Currency (Type 2) In the case of an independently defined ECU with a fixed but adjustable exchange rate vis-à-vis the community currencies, the development of the value of the parallel currency would be divorced from the development of the components forming the basket as it exists today but would depend on the frequency and extent of future realignments within the EMS. In principle, two possibilities exist as far as the exchange-rate regulations governing an independently defined ECU are concerned.

On the one hand, the ECU can be made superior to all EMS currencies by laying down the parities and intervention points of the national currencies vis-à-vis the ECU as the focal point of the system. Their bilateral central rates would then be derived from the ECU parity of each national currency with the consequence that the bilateral margin of fluctuation between two national currencies would be twice as large as it is vis-à-vis the ECU (for example, a band of $\pm 1^{1}/_{8}\%$ vis-à-vis the ECU would result in a bilateral band of $\pm 2^{1}/_{4}\%$). Thus, as a regional pivotal currency in the community, the ECU would play a similar role in formal terms as the U.S. dollar did in the former Bretton Woods system (without, however, having its own currency area as a base).

On the other hand, the independently defined ECU could be placed on the same footing as the national currencies; in this case, it would be treated as the currency of a thirteenth member country and would correspondingly have the same margin of fluctuation as the national currencies (whereby it could nevertheless be the focal point of the parity grid for computational purposes). Although the first variant would be of greater symbolic importance in the field of European politics and would foster the acceptance of the ECU as a parallel currency owing to its narrower margin of fluctuation, in principle both variants raise the same problems to a large extent.

As far as the ability of the ECU to crowd out other currencies is concerned, its being defined as an independent entity could potentially have both advantages and disadvantages because the new ECU could develop a priori more strongly than the strongest community currency but could also develop more weakly than the weakest community currency. In the absence of additional assumptions, such as equipping the parallel currency with a value guarantee (whereby, of course, only its use as an investment instrument but not as a borrowing instrument would be fostered) or assuring its usability worldwide, the ability of an independently defined ECU to crowd out other currencies as an investment instrument cannot be assessed conclusively. Ultimately, the decisive factor for the development of its value would be the extent to which ECUs are created by community authority (or by the national central banks of the community member countries in accordance with uniform community directives) in relation to the monetary demand for ECUs, which in turn would depend on the degree of acceptance of the ECU inside and outside the community.

As is the case with a national currency, independently defined ECUs would be put into circulation through credits granted by the issuing authority to banks or public sector entities as well as through purchases of partner currencies or third currencies via interventions on the foreign exchange markets. In the final analysis, the governing factor in this process would need to be the monetary demand for ECUs which results from the use of the ECU as a currency in cash transactions, settlement operations, and other payment transactions as well as for investment purposes in competition with each individual national currency.

It is of course difficult to assess according to which criteria such a monetary demand for ECUs would emerge. This would not least depend on how great the risk of a change in the value of ECU cash holdings is assessed to be in relation to holdings in national currency. Holding ECUs for transaction purposes would probably be a more attractive proposition in countries with a weak currency than in countries whose currencies tend to appreciate vis-à-vis the ECU. Economic agents in countries with a strong currency will at best hold ECUs for transaction purposes to the extent that they have to conclude and also settle contracts denominated in ECUs in intra-community trade and payment transactions for competitive reasons. The wide use of the ECU as a currency by residents as an investment and reserve currency both inside and outside the community would presuppose wide and deep markets as well as the willingness of bodies inside (and outside) the community that enjoy confidence to incur debt in the ECU as currency in a form and on conditions that appear advantageous to investors. However, a sufficient degree of acceptance on the part of investors—both inside and outside the community—is to be expected only if the creation of the ECU as an independent currency is carefully limited by the central bank(s) responsible for this task.

The granting of an excessive amount of ECU credits to the national or community fiscal authorities (for example, for transfer payments within the community) in particular could lead to an oversupply of ECUs and ultimately to a deterioration in the value of the ECU vis-à-vis national currencies in the community. This would not only impair the competitive position of the ECU in relation to the national currencies; owing to the obligations of the national central banks to intervene against the ECU, excess ECUs would also need to be taken out of the market by the central banks against national currency, which would make it difficult—if not impossible—for the countries concerned to conduct a monetary policy geared to stability. These risks to monetary policy would need to be assessed all the more carefully the more strongly the creation of ECUs were to be subject to political influences and the less flexible the exchange rate of the ECU were to be.

5. In the final analysis, a parallel currency strategy presupposes that the process whereby other currencies are crowded out through the free play of market forces actually does work. The requisite symmetrical substitution of all community currencies by the parallel currency would come about only if the parallel currency:

• were given the same domestic status as every other community currency;

• could compete even with the strongest community currency, taking interest rate and exchange-rate developments into account; and

• involved minimum costs as a transaction currency, which would practically be the case only if it were sufficiently firmly pegged to the national currencies.

However, this more or less amounts to a definition of the final stage to which the parallel currency is supposed to lead.

The interim solutions comprising either a basket ECU or an independently defined ECU with fixed, but adjustable exchange rates do not provide sufficient assurance that the process of integration would be free of tensions. On the contrary, they would involve the risk that national monetary policy would no longer be able to fulfill its mandate to ensure stability owing to larger-scale central bank interventions. In weighing the costs and benefits of a parallel currency strategy, it also needs to be taken into account that for day-to-day payment operations (cash transactions, settlement operations by machine, cashless payment transactions) a parallel currency would be entirely impractical. Ultimately, this leads to the conclusion that little would be gained politically by introducing a parallel currency but that much would be placed at risk in terms of stability policy.

C   A European Monetary Authority on the Way to a Single Currency

In the meantime, if the concept of a regional IMF that was behind the original plans to create the EMS appears to be obsolete and a European parallel currency is not an approach towards monetary union that deserves support, then it appears appropriate to prepare the prerequisites for introducing a single European currency at a later date by gradually harmonizing the national currencies in qualitative terms. Such a development could be brought about by extending the role of the EC committee of governors. In this context, it is not absolutely necessary for it to become the management body of an EC monetary authority equipped with operational tools immediately; it could also exercise the function of a central decisionmaking body within a community central bank system comprising the committee and the national central banks involved.

The committee of governors is particularly suitable for an extension of its functions because (in contrast, for example, to the administrative council of the EMCF) it is de jure free from instructions. Taking part in this committee, however, does not automatically annul the de facto dependence on instructions of individual governors that exists under national law. It would therefore be desirable if this dependence could be gradually eliminated as the functions of the committee are further extended and be replaced by increasing independence. As in the case of all other models, its mandate (maintaining the stability of money) and its status (freedom from instructions) should be assured at the outset.

Since the process of integration is to be seen as an evolutionary process, before decisionmaking responsibilities are transferred to supranational institutions, the question should be examined as to whether additional possibilities to extend coordination exist and in which direction they lie. Above all, further steps appear conceivable and would also be useful where the present forms of cooperation are based mainly on an ex post exchange of information (policy vis-à-vis third currencies, changes in the field of supervision, laying down the interim objectives of monetary policy, etc.,). They could gradually be developed into an *ex ante* exchange of information, such as is already occasionally practiced on an informal basis.

In principle, the activity of the committee of governors (the title of which could be changed in the course of this process to European central bank council, for instance, in order to emphasize its importance) would be directed toward coordinating national objectives, individual decisions, and the employment of monetary instruments. Based on current procedures, the degree of coordination could be gradually increased in the direction of obligatory advance consultations to the level of a kind of right to issue general directives.

In this way, the scope for national monetary policy action would be gradually reduced. It would, for example, encompass the pursuit of intermediate objectives adopted in the process of coordination or set later on as part of the power to issue directives. The scope for action would remain greatest in choosing appropriate instruments for achieving the objectives, but here again the committee would gain increasing influence over the course of time with the aim of gradually harmonizing the criteria on which the employment of certain instruments is based, extending to the creation of as uniform a set of instruments as possible.

As a kind of natural continuation of the tasks already undertaken by the committee at present with respect to the exchange rates of the community currencies in relation to each other and vis-à-vis third currencies, it would have to coordinate the intervention policy of the EC central banks with respect to the internal and external relationships of the community, with a sufficient degree of exchange-rate flexibility vis-à-vis third currencies being assured. In this context, account would need to be taken of the differing weights of the currencies within the EMS as well as their international role. Exchange-rate policy vis-à-vis the rest of the world would have to take into consideration the fact that the third countries concerned (the United States and

Japan) play a major role in determining the various exchange-rate relationships. At a later stage, the committee
could assume the responsibility for influencing exchange
rates, which is still a national preserve, so that in the event
of any foreign exchange market interventions, the national
central banks would progressively operate in the framework of their administering a mandate. The responsibility
for determining central rates could also be transferred from
the member governments to the committee. In this way,
there would be a greater scope for relevant decisions to be
asserted regardless of political expediency.

A committee of governors with scope to influence
exchange-rate policy and monetary policy in the member
countries could make an effective contribution to convergence that would foster integration. The objective behind
the basic thrust of its policy would need to be to influence
monetary policy in each member country in such a way
that a symmetrical development is brought about on the
basis of as great a degree of price stability as possible. The
success of such an undertaking is indivisibly associated
with comparable progress in terms of integration being
achieved in fiscal policy and other areas relevant to economic policy.

IV   Transitional Problems

A   Legal Basis

Competence in the field of economic and monetary policy
has not yet been transferred to the European Community.
The member states continue to be responsible for these
spheres of policy; however, they do have the commitment
to coordinate their policies (Section 2, 104, 105, and 145 of
the Treaty of Rome) in order to achieve their common ob-

jectives, to maintain a high level of employment and stability of the price level, to ensure equilibrium in the overall balance of payments, and to maintain confidence in their currencies (Section 104 of the Treaty of Rome). A certain restriction for the member countries through community law is seen in the fact that they should consider their exchange-rate policies as a matter of common interest (Section 107 of the Treaty of Rome).

Restrictions that go further result from the rules governing the EMS. Leaving aside two council directives relating to the EMCF and the ECU, they are based on multilaterally agreed acts of self-restriction on the part of the central banks concerned and hence are not part of the legislation of the community proper. In accordance with a regulation in respect of the treaty (Section 102(a) of the Treaty of Rome) introduced together with the Single European Act of 1986, institutional changes in the field of economic and monetary policy undertaken in the course of further developments require the conclusion of a new treaty under international law in accordance with Section 236 of the Treaty of Rome. How far an international treaty is necessary in individual cases depends on the scope each central bank has in extending economic policy cooperation under its basis in law. This probably differs from country to country since the central banks in the individual member countries have a differing status in law.

No definitive catalogue can be drawn up for Germany indicating what acts of legislation would be required in each case for measures that are designed to further develop the EMS. In abstract terms, the following guidelines can be set forth:

1. In Germany, under Section 24 of the Basic Law, the transfer of sovereign rights to international institutions requires an act of parliament. This requirement of constitutional law is to be

interpreted strictly (Federal Constitutional Law 58, p.1ff., and especially p. 35).

2. The Deutsche Bundesbank is able to participate in closer monetary policy cooperation through greater cooperation among central banks only within certain limits. A limit would be reached if the Bundesbank were to accept decisions by an external body—such as the committee of governors—with respect to monetary policy measures which it is its duty to decide upon autonomously. In doing so, it would relinquish the exercise of the authority it has under the Bundesbank act. German public and administrative law assumes that a body that has been entrusted with tasks and responsibilities exercises these responsibilities directly; delegating them to another body is only possible if it is empowered to do so by law. It is also not permissible for such a body to link the decisions entrusted to it to the agreement of other bodies. In contrast, mutual agreements and concertations are and remain possible.

3. The Deutsche Bundesbank is not able to establish a joint institution together with other central banks and grant it powers in the field of monetary policy either; for this, owing to the lack of the necessary authorization, it does not have the power of organization required under public law.

4. Finally, on the basis of existing law, the Deutsche Bundesbank cannot transfer parts or all of its monetary reserves permanently and irrevocably to a common fund; such a transfer would go beyond the scope of the operations the bank is empowered to conduct.)

Before national responsibilities are transferred to the community, sufficient clarity should exist as to the distribution of responsibilities at the community level. The point behind this is to ensure that the principles of a European monetary order as described above have been put into effect at least in basic terms at every stage of integration. With respect to the position of the community monetary authorities, this means that no rights of any kind to issue instructions are granted to the political level and that an influence on national central banks does not accrue to the national political authorities to which they do not have a right under national law. This would speak in favor of making the committee of EC central bank governors, which is free from political instructions both at the national and the community level, the starting point for further development in institutional terms. The members of this committee would need to enjoy personal independence from the bodies that appoint them, which admittedly also presupposes corresponding independence in their functions at the national level. In contrast, the EMCF, which is tied to directives issued by the EC council of ministers and hence is subject to political instructions, is not suitable as a monetary authority for the community.

B   Integration in Stages

Whether responsibilities in the field of monetary policy can be transferred to the community level in several steps or in a single act of law depends on the concept on which the integration process is based. In principle, preference should be given to a global concept of integration with a clearly formulated final objective, as described above, with the individual states being geared to this objective. A process of integration determined only by pragmatic considerations would not offer any guarantee that the final objective will actually be attained. It would be in accordance with this global concept of integration if the necessary authorization were not to be restricted to individual steps in the process of integration but were to relate to the stage-by-stage plan as a whole, or at least to its major components. The member countries applied this procedure successfully in bringing about the customs union in the first decade of the community's existence. However, experience with the Werner plan of 1970 to achieve economic and monetary union in stages argues against setting a rigid timetable for the process of integration. Rather, institutional changes, which also include extensions in the spheres of competence of existing community institutions, should be made dependent on qualitative progress toward convergence in the field of economic and monetary policy. The member countries would, of course, need to agree on a common procedure to determine whether the prerequisites have been fulfilled for the next stage toward economic and monetary union to be put into effect.

From a legal point of view, the establishment of an economic and monetary union in the community does not depend on the existence of a political union. Rather, it is an accepted fact that the member countries of the community can separate certain tasks from the multitude of responsibilities they have and transfer them to a supranational institution. They nevertheless continue to exist as states. They continue to pursue their own policies in major fields and have the necessary executive power to do so (territorial and individual sovereignty). To this extent, the jointly created supranational entity—in this case, the European Community—exists as an association for the specific purpose of integrating certain functions.

As was already stated in the Werner Report of 1970, a lasting economic and monetary union requires the transfer of far-reaching responsibilities of national authorities to the community plane above and beyond the direct field of monetary policy. An association for the specific purpose of integrating certain functions would therefore probably only be able to survive if it is supported by a far-reaching re-shaping of the community in political and institutional terms in the direction of a more comprehensive union. To this extent, progress toward economic, monetary, and general political union is mutually interdependent and thus establishes the framework in which progress in institutional terms appears possible.

C   Partial Integration Versus Comprehensive Integration

Important political considerations can also plead against integration by stages where individual groups of countries move toward integration at varying speeds. Endeavors therefore should be made to include all the community member countries in the process of monetary integration. So long as considerable differentials exist within the community in terms of prosperity and productivity that are not offset to a large extent and in good time through corresponding transfers of resources in the context of fiscal compensation within the union, movements in the factors of production among the various regions can occur as internal market conditions are brought about. The more developed regions will be given impulses to growth at the expense of the periphery. To the extent that they do not prefer to allow themselves to be guided by general political considerations, this risk will probably deter a number of member countries of the community from joining a monetary union. In contrast, a core group of countries, such as those comprising the members of the present EMS exchange-rate system, appear to be quite strong enough in economic terms to agree to closer and closer ties with corresponding consequences in the field of economic policy.

The concept of integration by stages was practiced under the snake system and is practiced de facto within the EMS. Since monetary policy coordination largely took place in these systems up to now on a cooperative basis, the coexistence of differing rights and obligations in various countries did not impair cooperation. If, however, substantial progress toward integration is tied to major institutional bonds, individual countries by exercising their veto could bring about a situation where such progress is made only on the basis of the lowest common denominator. The countries capable of integrating could escape this situation by agreeing on more rapid steps toward integration among themselves. In this case, the countries at the lower level of integration would no longer be able to participate in the monetary policy decisionmaking bodies of the community on an equal basis as is the case at the present level of cooperation by means of a gentlemen's agreement. Only the countries prepared to subject themselves to its standards could have a claim to participate fully in the monetary union.

Integration by stages would be tantamount to dividing the community into two parts which would not remain restricted to the monetary sphere as integration progressed but would also lead to the individual member countries of the community having different rights and obligations. Although such a system of differing rights and obligations in individual spheres would not be considered to be incompatible with the Treaty of Rome, independent bodies of the monetary union would need to be created alongside the organs of the community in order to meet the demands of the final objective. In light of the present state of development of the European Community, this division between the level of cooperation and the level of integration would not only raise serious problems of a practical nature but the unification of Europe would gain a new quality through the partial integration of a number of core member countries as compared with the approach to integration adopted in the past. New hurdles would be raised for the countries on the periphery that would be increasingly difficult to overcome. The proponents of faster integration of the core member countries see this primarily as a transitional problem; they argue that, with the system being open to a corresponding extent, the countries initially excluded from this process could catch up with the train of integration later on when the economic prerequisites to do so have been created. However, the danger must not be dismissed that ultimately the differences between the member countries in economic terms will become cemented with the division of Europe into two parts in the field of monetary policy and in the related institutions. Although the pull of an incipient monetary union would be strong for the countries on the periphery, the high barriers of access to it might possibly frustrate their joining it, in the long run. If the unification of Europe as a whole is also being striven for, then two-speed integration in the monetary sphere would tend to an obstacle.

D   Integration Under the Treaty of Rome or Outside It

The stage-by-stage plan together with the description of the individual steps up to the final stage could be decided upon in a single package and extend the Treaty of Rome by the dimension comprising economic and monetary union. This package solution would have the advantage that it would be the subject of forming a political opinion in all the member countries only once and that it would not be necessary to negotiate the union several times over in small coin before the national legislative bodies, apart from the imponderables of the producer as arose with the ratification of the Single European Act.

Through a package solution of this nature, not only would the objectives be laid down in contractual form but the requisite responsibilities of the community would also be established. As a result, the issuing of regulations in unforeseen circumstances under Section 235 of the Treaty of Rome would no longer be necessary. Disagreements would be excluded on the issue, for instance, as to when institutional changes occur (see Section 102(a)) or whether a measure in the field of monetary policy is still accessible to extensive interpretation under Section 235.

If, in the context of such an extended treaty, a decision-making body decides to conclude one stage of integration and initiates the next step in monetary policy cooperation, then the question arises as to which body should be granted this responsibility. Several solutions to this question are conceivable. The treaty already entrusts the council with the authority to take decisions on such determinations in other cases (see, for example, the determination of the council with respect to the transitional period; Section 8 of the Treaty of Rome). In principle, the commission could also be entrusted with making such a determination. As regards the technical expertise involved, however, the committee of central bank governors could also be considered for this task. A mixed body is conceivable as well.

If it is assumed, however, that not all the member countries enter the integrational stage in the field of monetary policy at the same time, it will hardly be possible to grant these member countries the right to participate in its design. The countries engaged in the process of integration will not want to expose themselves to the risk of being partly governed by outsiders and expect that only those countries take part that expose themselves to the same risk. For this reason, it could prove necessary to lay down the corresponding rules among the active participants outside the Treaty of Rome initially. Basically speaking this route was taken with the inception of the EMS. It would avoid the systematics of the Treaty of Rome and make monetary integration within the framework of the committee of governors possible, which correspond to the basic feature of a European monetary order described above. At a later stage, ways would need to be discussed on how to harmonize the new set of rules with the Treaty of Rome.

The objection could be raised against bringing about monetary integration outside the Treaty of Rome that this approach would not correspond to the final objective of creating an economic and monetary union within the community. Under Section 102(a), it could be argued, member countries have undertaken a mandatory commitment to adopt the procedure laid down in Section 236 of the Treaty of Rome when they enter the institutional stage. They would have to refrain from all measures that could jeopardize the achievement of the objectives laid down in the Treaty of Rome (Section 5, Subsection 2). The commission will also have a considerable interest in incorporating the monetary policy institutions in the Treaty of Rome.

If the route prescribed under Section 236 of the Treaty of Rome is taken, then the entry into force of changes in the treaty is made dependent on their being ratified by all the member countries. An individual member country would then be in a position to prevent the institutionalization of cooperation, or at least to delay it considerably.

V Concluding Remarks

Since the inception of the EMS considerable progress has been made in the community in the field of monetary policy cooperation. In conjunction with the latest measures to establish an integrated financial area and the planned establishment of the single European market, the perspective of an economic and monetary union now appears in a favorable light again. Economic and monetary union would mark the end of a development which, despite all the considerable progress that has been made, will still take some time to achieve. Not all the member countries of the community participate in the exchange-rate mechanism of the EMS, and not all the participating countries subject themselves to the same conditions. The economic prerequisites for a monetary union that is characterized by immutably fixed exchange rates between the participating countries will probably not exist for the foreseeable future. Even among the members who form the nucleus of the exchange-rate system, tensions must repeatedly be expected for the foreseeable future owing to differing economic policy preferences and constraints as well as the resultant divergences in their economic development, which will make realignments in central rates of their currencies necessary. Even within a common single market these problems will not simply disappear, especially seeing that this market will trigger additional structural adjustment constraints, the extent of which cannot as yet be fully assessed. For this reason, too, it will not be possible to do fully without occasional realignments in central rates for the foreseeable future. This indicates the necessity for further progress in the direction of greater convergence in a large number of macroeconomic as well as structural fields.

The existing EC committee of central bank governors offers itself as the basic unit in organizational terms of an EC monetary authority that does not threaten to run counter to the demands of the final stage at the outset. Competence in the field of monetary policy could be increasingly transferred to it over time. In the initial stages it would direct its activities toward coordinating national monetary policy objectives, individual decisions, and the employment of monetary policy instruments. Parallel to this, it would ensure an increasingly greater degree of harmonization of the exchange-rate policies of the member countries. Working from this basis, its responsibilities could gradually be extended in the direction of obligatory advance consultations and go as far as having the right to issue directives on questions of monetary and exchange-rate policy. A major factor in coordinating monetary policy at the community level is the centralized process of reshaping policy, which could be undertaken by the national central banks as the constituent parts of a European central bank system. In organizational terms, the committee of governors could be supported by its own enlarged secretariat.

Developing its own activities in the money and foreign exchange markets on the part of an EC monetary authority equipped with technical resources and staff as well as monetary policy instruments would not appear to be necessary until the national currencies have been abolished and a single European currency has been introduced. The step-by-step transition from a national to a community monetary policy should take place on a legal basis that does not relate to individual steps in the process of integration but to this process as a whole. As far as possible, all the member countries of the community should embark jointly on the path toward economic and monetary union in order not to handicap the integration of Europe as a whole at a later date.

If only a few community member countries were to spur forward this would have serious economic and political consequences. Ultimately, the danger would exist of Western Europe being permanently divided into two parts if the barriers to access to the smaller system were to become too high. However, to the extent that separate action in Europe were politically desired, the door would have to be left open for the countries excluded in the initial stages to join later. But these countries could not be granted any right to participate in the affairs of the monetary union. Besides institutional arrangements of this nature, however, it is of outstanding importance for the success of monetary integration for the gradual transfer of monetary policy to the community level to be accompanied by sufficient progress in the integration of economic and fiscal policy. Isolated steps in the monetary field would overburden monetary policy in political terms and jeopardize the credibility of the process of unification in the longer run.

Index